THE HARRIER

The World's First
V/STOL Fighter

David Oliver

AMBERLEY

First published 2018

Amberley Publishing
The Hill, Stroud, Gloucestershire, GL5 4EP
www.amberley-books.com

Copyright © David Oliver, 2018

The right of David Oliver to be identified as the
Author of this work has been asserted in accordance with
the Copyright, Designs and Patents Act 1988.

ISBN 978 1 4456 5041 8 (print)
ISBN 978 1 4456 5042 5 (ebook)

British Library Cataloguing in Publication Data.
A catalogue record for this book is available from the
British Library.

Origination by Amberley Publishing.
Printed in Great Britain.

Contents

Introduction

Since the dawn of the jet age, designers had been experimenting with vertical take-off and landing fighter aircraft, most of which were limited by the technologies of the time and ended in failure. It was the combination of Hawker Siddeley's chief designer, Sir Sydney Camm, and Sir Stanley Hooker, the technical director of Bristol Aero Engines, who together had the vision to design and build the world's first successful vertical/short take-off and landing (V/STOL) fighter aircraft.

Under development since 1957, when design work was initiated by Hawker Siddeley as a private venture, the P1127, subsequently named the Kestrel, was the world's first jet-powered V/STOL strike and reconnaissance fighter. It was designed around the unique Bristol Siddeley Pegasus turbofan engine developed by Gordon Lewis, who was inspired by the French engineer Michel Wibault's lift/thrust engine concept. The Pegasus was basically an Orpheus driving a two-stage ducted fan, discharging air through two pairs of nozzles mechanically connected together and capable of rotation to permit all the installed thrust to be vectored to match the demands of vertical or short take-off and landing at one end of the scale and climb acceleration and level speed at the other. The design of the Kestrel was crystallised by 1958 as a relatively simple, single-seat tactical strike and reconnaissance fighter as a potential replacement for the Royal Air Force (RAF) Hawker Hunter in the ground attack role, but more specifically as a 'third generation' NATO lightweight strike and reconnaissance aircraft.

The Kestrel was designed as the forerunner of the heavier and much more powerful P1154 that was to be developed for the RAF as a successor to the Hunter. The supersonic P1154 was to be powered by the Bristol Siddeley BS100 vectorable turbofan delivering a maximum of 27,000 lb thrust, and a detailed design submission to ARS.356 was made in August 1954; a development order for eight aircraft was placed on February 1964. The first was to fly two years later, with service deliveries expected to begin in 1968. The technical winner of the abortive NATO Basic Military Requirement (BMR) 3 contest, the P1154 was to possess dual intercept-ground attack capability.

However, as Hawker Siddeley began building the first batch of aircraft, the new Labour government suddenly cancelled the project on 2 February 1965 on the ground of cost, to be replaced by the McDonnell Douglas Phantom F-4 in the intercept role and a new ground attack aircraft based on the Kestrel, named the Harrier.

The world's first VTOL fighter, the iconic Harrier, was designed to fight the Cold War from the fields of West Germany but won its battle spurs thousands of miles away in the Falklands, Belize and Afghanistan, until, as with the supersonic P1154, it was unceremoniously scrapped by the British government fifty years after entering service with the RAF.

Today the AV-8B Harrier II remains in frontline operations in Afghanistan and in the battle against ISIL forces in Syria, not with the RAF, but with the US Marine Corps (USMC), while the V/STOL fighter concept pioneered by the P1127/Kestrel/Harrier family is to be continued with the introduction of the supersonic Lockheed Martin F-35B Lightning II Joint Strike Fighter (JSF) into RAF and US Marine Corps service.

Above: The fifth Hawker Siddeley prototype P1127 experimental vertical/short take-off and landing (V/STOL) aircraft, XP980, during an early hover test flight. (BAE Systems)

Below: Royal Air Force Hawker Siddeley Harrier GR.1s of the newly formed No. 20 Squadron in 1970. (BAE Systems)

Above: Joint Force Harrier GR.7 ZD327 over Afghanistan on an Operation *Herrick* mission in 2006. (No. 1 Squadron archives)

Below: The Harrier's S/VTOL successor, an RAF Lockheed Martin F-35B Lightning II, leads a US Marine Corps aircraft in 2016. (Crown Copyright)

CHAPTER 1

Flight of the Kestrel

In 1958 the Hawker project office under Sir Sydney Camm began the development of a unique vertical and/or short take-off and landing (V/STOL) strike aircraft as a private venture intended as a replacement for the ground attack variants of the Royal Air Force (RAF) Hawker Hunter. Support was subsequently obtained from the British Ministry of Aviation with an order for six P1127 prototypes and a 75 per cent financial backing for the Bristol Siddeley engine. The first drawings for the P1127 were issued to the experimental shop in May 1959 and construction of the first aircraft occupied approximately eighteen months. The Hawker Siddeley chief test pilot, A. W. 'Bill' Bedford, made the first hovering trials at Dunsford on 21 October 1960 , first with the aircraft tethered and then in free flight. It was then taken to the RAE at Bedford for, on 13 March 1961, conventional forward take-off and flight, with nozzles kept in the position for maximum forward thrust. The next stage of the flight trials was initiated at Dunsfold, where the first prototype, XP831, was joined on 5 July 1961 by the second P1127, XP836. Early in September 1961 full transitions from vertical to horizontal flight mode and back were made.

Stanley Hooker of Bristol Siddeley was responsible for the power of the P1127 and, along with aero-engine designer Gordon Lewis, was predominantly responsible for the creation of the Pegasus engine and its use in the vectored-thrust project. The aircraft had two large air intakes to the compressor and four individual jet outlets – two on each side of the engine – that could be rotated 90 degrees so that the jet thrust could be used to give the aircraft vertical lift or horizontal thrust. As the total aircraft weight was less than the total 12,500 lb thrust developed by the unique Bristol Siddeley Pegasus 2 engine, the P1127 was capable of vertical take-off. Once the aircraft was airborne, the jet nozzles were gradually rotated until the whole engine thrust was being used for forward flight. The two forward nozzles ejected cold air from the two-stage front fan while the rear nozzles were used for the hot exhaust from the turbine.

For normal forward flight, the P1127 had conventional control surfaces, ailerons, an all-moving slab tailplane and a rudder. As these surfaces were not effective when the aircraft had little or no forward

Hawker Chief Test Pilot Bill Bedford flew one of the early tethered hovering tests with the P1127 prototype XP831 at Dunsfold in October 1960. (Francois Prins archive)

P1127 XP972 started test flying in April 1962 but was destroyed on 30 October 1962 while the test pilot attempted an emergency landing at RAF Tangmere when the engine failed. (Francois Prins archive)

Three P1127 prototypes seen on 7 June 1963. From the top: XP980, flown by Hugh Merewether, XP976, flown by Duncan Simpson, and XP831, flown by Bill Bedford. (Francois Prins archive)

The fourth P1127 prototype, XP980, conducting open field landing trials. (Rolls-Royce)

speed, there was a secondary system for pitch, yaw and roll control by means of small wingtip nozzles, and under the fuselage, nose and tail. Another unique feature for low speed hovering flight was an inflatable lip around each intake, which ensured adequate airflow at low speeds but which could be deflated for higher speeds when ram effect achieved a similar result. A zero speed, zero height Martin Baker ejection seat was developed for the P1127.

Over the next three years the five prototypes conducted performance trials, during which they achieved Mach 1.0 in shallow dives, weapons tests carrying 250 lb practice bombs, and deck trials on the carrier HMS *Ark Royal*.

Following financial support from the US Mutual Weapons Development Programme, the Ministry of Aviation placed a contract for two (later six) development militarised derivatives of the P1127, known as the Kestrel. The first aircraft, XS688, flew for the first time on 7 March, powered by a 15,500 lb thrust Pegasus 5 vectored thrust turbofan engine.

A service test batch of nine Kestrel FGA.1 aircraft was ordered for use by a joint British–US–German trials squadron, the Tripartite Evaluation Squadron (TES), based at RAF West Raynham, which included pilots and ground crew from the UK, USA and West Germany. The previous experience of the ten TES pilots varied considerably with experienced RAF, USN and USAF fast jets pilots, US Army

Hawker P1127 XS688, preserved at the Fleet Air Arm Museum at Yeovilton. (Francois Prins)

Flying the P1127 prototype XP831, Bill Bedford made the first deck landing on HMS *Ark Royal* on 8 February 1963. (Francois Prins archive)

The first Hawker Siddeley Kestrel F(GA) Mk.1, XS688 made its first flight on 7 March 1964. (Francois Prins archive)

The simple layout of the Kestrel F(GA) Mk.1 (Francois Prins)

pilots with several thousand hours flying on helicopters but no experience of fast jets, and Col Gerhard Barkhorn – the second highest scoring Luftwaffe ace of the Second World War.

The evaluation aircraft, known as the 'Tripartite Nine', embodied a number of modifications from the P1127 that were included when the first example flew on 7 March 1964. They differed from the prototypes by having a camera nose and four stores under-wing pylons, powered by a 15,200 lb thrust Pegasus 5 and flying at Mach 0.8 with maximum fuel, with 10 per cent reserves over a maximum ferry range of 2,350 miles and a 220-mile radius of action for a low-level sortie at 500 ft.

During its operations in 1965, the TES pilots used nearby abandoned airfields for testing the aircraft on semi-prepared runways and on grass to test its capabilities on unprepared sites. At the end of the trials, the TES pilots had flown 960 sorties and carried out 1,366 take-offs and landings without incident. One of the Kestrel FGA.1s, XS695, now preserved at Royal Air Force Museum Cosford, flew 141 sorties with the TES, and during 1966 appeared at the Farnborough and Hanover Air Shows. In 1972 it was allocated to the Royal Navy Engineering College at Manadon, Devon, being used for apprentice training and to simulate aircraft handling and flight deck procedures.

The second P1127 prototype, XP972, wearing the tripartite makings of the UK, USA and Germany. (Francois Prins archive)

A Kestrel F(GA) Mk.1 seen in the markings of the Tripartite Evaluation Squadron (TES), formed on 1 April 1965 at RAF West Raynham. (Francois Prins archive)

Seen in RAF marking and carrying rocket pods, after flying with the TES, Kestrel XS695 was used for training and appeared at the Hanover and Farnborough Air Shows. (Francois Prins archive)

Six of the trials aircraft were subsequently transferred to the United States where they were designated XV-6As for additional testing by the US Armed Forces. The success of the unique Tripartite Squadron trials proved the validity of the vectored thrust principle for military tactical purposes and led, ultimately, to the introduction of the fully militarised Harrier.

Kestrel F(GA). Mk.1 XS695, which flew 141 sorties with the TES in 1965, is on display at the RAF Museum Cosford. (Francois Prins)

Operated by NASA for ship-landing trials, XV-6A 64-18266 was former Kestrel F(GA) Mk.1 XS692, which is now preserved at the Air Power Park and Museum a Hampton, Virginia. (NASA)

Above: XV-6A 64-18262, preserved at the United States Air Force Museum at Wright-Patterson, Dayton, Ohio, was a former TES Kestrel F(GA) Mk.1, XS688. (USAF)

Below: Former TES Kestrel F(GA) Mk.1 XS689 became a trials aircraft with NASA before being preserved at the Virginia Air and Space Center. (NASA)

CHAPTER 2

Cold War Warriors

The Kestrel FGA.1 was a subsonic design that was intended to have been followed by a supersonic V/STOL development, the P1154, which was the intended RAF Hawker Hunter replacement. However, in 1964 the P1154 was cancelled as an economy measure by the Labour government, which proved to be very costly for not only the RAF, but also for the British aerospace industry. The P1154 was to have been powered by the 33,000 lb thrust Bristol Siddeley BS100 engine and would have been capable of Mach 2.3 at altitude and Mach 1.2 at sea level. By contrast, the Hawker Harrier GR.1, a militarised development of the Kestrel FGA.1 introduced into RAF service as a less costly alternative to the P1154, remained subsonic in level flight. The first of six development Harriers, XV276 was flown on 31 August 1966, and the first production aircraft, XV738, on 28 December 1967.

Despite its superficial resemblance to the earlier Kestrel, the Harrier had undergone extensive redesign to accommodate a more powerful Rolls-Royce Pegasus turbofan, a more sophisticated navigation/attack system, increased fuel tankage, a detachable in-flight refueling probe and an increased life airframe.

It was introduced into front-line RAF service when the Harrier was issued to No. 1(F) Squadron at RAF Wittering in July 1969. With its unique ability of vertical take-off, hovering in front of crowds and vertical landing, the Harrier soon became much in demand at air shows in the UK and abroad. During May 1969, a Harrier GR.1 took part in the *Daily Mail* Trans-Atlantic Air Race, starting with a spectacular take-off from St Pancras station in central London and landing in central New York after a flight of 6 hours and 11 minutes, a feat achieved with air-refuelling over the Atlantic.

Duncan Simpson, who carried out a great deal of the test flying of P1127/Kestrel and Harrier, is seen here with a modified Harrier GR.1 and an array of Marconi black boxes and radar equipment. (Francois Prins archive)

An early production Hawker Siddeley Harrier GR.Mk.1 making a vertical take-off and carrying a single 1,000 lb bomb. (Francois Prins archive)

Harrier GR.1 XV740 carrying two Matra 155 rocket launchers, seen hovering with the undercarriage and airbrake extended. (Francois Prins archive)

Harrier GR.1 XV744, piloted by Squadron Leader Tom Lecky-Thompson, at St Pancras station in central London on 5 May 1969 after winning the *Daily Mail* Trans-Atlantic Air Race to New York. (BAE Systems)

The revolutionary ground attack aircraft was tailor-made for the RAF Germany (RAFG) role with its ability to operate from forest hides and lift-off from unprepared airstrips in short take-off and vertical landing (STOVL) mode in support of NATO forces. No. IV(AC) Squadron bought its Harrier GR.1s to RAF Wildenrath in West Germany in June 1970 to work up the role after re-equipping at RAF Wittering.

For nearly a year it was the only Harrier unit in RAFG, the second squadron being No. 20, which was reformed on 1 December also at Wildenrath. The two-squadron Wing soon became fully operational, converting to the GR.1A, and then the GR.3 in the next eighteen months. On 1 January 1972 the Wing was completed by the re-formed No. 3 Squadron at Wildenrath.

However, the GR.1 had been underpowered and difficult to fly. The tailfin had no directional control below 90 knots, and when in transition speeds between 30 and 90 knots were difficult as there appeared to be more lift on one side of the aircraft than the other, which could cause the aircraft to lose stability. Although the Harriers underwent a series of phased improvements after entering service, including being updated to GR.1As by being re-engined with Pegasus 102 engines, ten early Harriers were written off in accidents. The final update was to GR.3 standard with the 21.500 lb thrust Rolls-Royce Pegasus 103. Bristol Siddeley had merged with Rolls-Royce Ltd in 1968, which also featured the Marconi laser ranging and marked target seeking (LRMTS) fitted in a thimble added to the nose. Already equipped with a Ferranti FE.541 Inertial Navigation and Attack System (INAS) and the Smiths Industries Head-Up Display (HUD). A forward Marconi ARI 18223 E-J band radar-warning receiver (RWR) was added to the fin and another to the extreme rear fuselage. The Harrier carried a single oblique camera in the port side of the nose and could be equipped with a reconnaissance pod on the centerline pylon with a Forward F135 camera, port and starboard F95 Mk.7 cameras and a signal data converter.

With a 5,000 lb weapons payload, the Harrier GR.3's armament included twin 30 mm Aden cannon in ventral strake pods plus weapon combinations of free-fall, cluster, retarded or 'smart' bombs, Matra rocket launchers with 68 mm SNEB rockets or Royal Navy 2-inch rockets, and AIM-9 Sidewinder air-to-air missiles. Two 100 imperial gallon auxiliary tanks could be carried on the inboard under-wing pylons.

In the Central Region the RAF Germany Harrier concept was entitled WARLOC, an abbreviation of war locations, evolved after 1970 when the first No. IV (AC) Squadron's Harriers arrived at RAF Wildenrath, one of the modern NATO 'Clutch' airfields west of Mönchengladbach. Within two years Nos 20 and 3 Squadrons had followed to form the thirty-six-aircraft RAF Germany Harrier Force that, in transition to war, would have been reinforced by up to twelve aircraft and pilots from the Harrier OCU at Wittering. The force had the option of operating from the main base at Wildenrath using the runway, parallel taxiways, revetment access tracks and a few nearby road strips, but the preferred concept was WARLOC, which was a complicated plan to deploy the Harrier Force forward to locations within the 1(BR) Corps area of responsibility. On 28 February 1977, after five years as a three-squadron Wing, No. 20 Squadron was split into two and added, one half each, to Nos 3 and IV (AC) Squadrons before moving to RAF Gütersloh a week later.

However, the RAF Harrier was to prove itself in combat, not in RAFG, but when fourteen GR.3s were deployed to the Falkland Islands in 1982, and subsequently in the defence of Belize.

Following their operational deployments, in May 1985 five Harrier GR.3s from No. 1(F) Squadron at RAF Wittering, with a seventy-strong detachment, again operated from HMS *Invincible* in a regular exercise to practice offensive air support of forces ashore from RN aircraft carriers. On 18 September Harrier GR.3s from Nos 3 and IV (AC) Squadrons at RAF Gütersloh participated in Exercise *Cold Fire*, operating for the first time ever from a German autobahn, demonstrating their ability to use 2 km of one lane of the road as a landing strip.

The Harrier GR.3 remained in service with RAFG until it was replaced by the GR.5 in March 1989, just as the Cold War was coming to a peaceful end. Of a total of 114 Harrier GR.1/3s delivered to the RAF, plus an additional three for replacement of Falklands loses, no less than sixty-one were written off.

No. IV (Army
Cooperation)
Squadron Harrier
GR.1A XV807
at the hover
carrying five
600 lb BL755
cluster bombs.
(BAE Systems)

British Aerospace
Harrier GR.3
XZ131, belonging
to No. IV (Army
Cooperation)
Squadron,
carrying a
multi-sensor
recce pod in the
hover over a
landing pad in
West Germany.
(Francois
Prins archive)

Harrier GR.3
XZ138 served
with No. 1 (F)
Squadron at
RAF Wittering
and took part
in the Falklands
campaign.
(Francois
Prins archive)

Harrier GR.3s
of No. 1 (F)
Squadron in a
temporary winter
camouflage
during a
NATO exercise
in Norway.
(BAE Systems)

One of the
LRMTS-equipped
two-seat Harrier
T.Mk.4s issued
to operational
RAFG squadrons
in a forest hide
in West Germany.
(Francois
Prins archive)

No. 20 Squadron Harrier GR.1 XV798, modified to GR.3 standard, firing a volley of 68 mm SNEB rockets during a live fire exercise. (Francois Prins archive)

The Harrier GR.3 production line at the Hawker Siddeley, later British Aerospace, factory at Kingston upon Thames. (Francois Prins archive)

A Harrier GR.3 making a short take-off (STO) from a roadway at Eberhard in North Germany. (Francois Prins archive)

Harrier GR.3 XZ136 was used for ski-jump trials and is seen here carrying a full load on the 500th ski-jump. (Francois Prins archive)

A Harrier GR.3, seen here firing 68 mm rockets from its Matra launcher, as identified by the Ferranti laser ranging and marked seeker in the nose. (BAE Systems)

A Harrier GR.3 belonging to the No. 233 OCU, which is armed with the twin 30 mm Aden cannon in ventral pods, and two Matra 18x68 mm rocket launchers. (David Oliver)

A No. 223 OCU Harrier GR.3 kicks up the grass during a demonstration at the Brands Hatch motor racing circuit. (David Oliver)

A pair of Harrier GR.1s of No. 1 (Fighter) Squadron on a field deployment exercise at RAF Gütersloh in 1972. (BAE Systems)

No. 3 Squadron Harrier GR.3 XV792, based at RAF Gütersloh in West Germany, makes a vertical landing. (Francois Prins archive)

The author in the back seat of a Harrier T.Mk.4, of No. 233 OCU at RAF Wittering, at low level over Lincolnshire. (Dennis J. Calvert)

Russian Yakovlev test pilot Vladimir Yakimov (left) after a flight in a No. 233 OCU Harrier T.Mk.4 with Falklands veteran Flt-Lt Jeff Glover. (Crown Copyright)

A total of sixty-two RAF Harrier GR.1/3 aircraft were written-off between October 1970 and May 1992. (Crown Copyright)

With the high attrition rate of early Harriers, there was an urgent requirement for a two-seat version and the first of two prototypes flew at Dunsfold on 24 April 1969. Twenty-four Harrier T.2 and T.4s were delivered to the RAF from July 1970. With the arrival of the Harrier T.2 in October 1970, No. 233 Operational Conversion Unit (OCU) was established at RAF Wittering, absorbing Harrier Conversion Team (HCT) at Dunsfold and started full operational conversions for first tourists.

The two-seat Harrier was identical in equipment and weapon delivery capability to the single-seat versions, but introduced an extra bay in the forward fuselage, and a lengthened fairing for the rear reaction control pipe to compensate for the longer nose. The fin height was later increased. The original T.2, powered by the Pegasus 101 turbofans, were upgraded to T.2A standard with the Pegasus 102 and to the T.4 with the 21.500 lb thrust Pegasus 103. Upgrading by the addition of LRMTS and RWR equipment followed in parallel with the single-seat Harriers. The last Harrier T.4 was delivered in March 1983. While most were delivered to No. 233 OCU, a small number were also issued to the four operational Harrier squadrons.

A formation of No. 233 Operational Conversion Unit, (OCU) based at RAF Wittering, armed with 30 mm Aden cannon pods and four Matra rocket launchers. (Francois Prins archive)

Built in 1970, Harrier T Mk.52 G-VTOL, the British Aerospace two-seat V/STOL company demonstrator, is preserved at the Brooklands Museum. (David Oliver)

CHAPTER 3

Harrier Gains its Sea Legs

A single-seat shipboard V/STOL multi-role fighter derived from the Hawker Siddeley Kestrel via the Harrier close support and tactical reconnaissance aircraft, the Sea Harrier was the result of initial project studies completed early in 1972 by Hawker Siddeley. A decision to proceed to full development of the P1184 and its Ferranti Blue Fox radar was announced on 15 May 1975. The first of twenty-four Sea Harrier FRS.1s was flown at Dunsfold on 28 August 1978, by which time Hawker Siddeley had been absorbed into British Aerospace (BAe). Compared with the RAF aircraft, the Sea Harrier had an airframe protected against saltwater corrosion with no magnesium parts, a raised cockpit, revised avionics and a folding nose radome. The 21,500 lb thrust Rolls-Royce Pegasus 104 vectored-thrust turbofan also had corrosion protection and generated more electrical power. The Fighter, Reconnaissance, Strike (FRS) Mk.1 Sea Harrier had provision for wing-pylon-mounted Sidewinder AIM-9 AAMs plus two Sea Eagle anti-ship missiles (ASMs). Two 30 mm Aden cannon pods could be attached under the fuselage.

BAe Sea Harrier FRS.Mk.12 XZ450 on a pre-delivery flight over British Aerospace airfield at Dunsfold, later serving No. 800 Naval Air Squadron (NAS). (BAE Systems)

Sea Harrier FRS.1 XZ454 showing its twin 30 mm Aden cannon pods and AIM-9 Sidewinder air-to-air missiles. (BAE Systems)

Trials were conducted with Sea Harrier FRS.1 XZ438 carrying a pair of British Aerospace Sea Eagle anti-ship missiles. (BAE Systems)

An early production Sea Harrier FRS.1, XZ492 of No. 800 NAS, is carrying cannon pods and Sidewinder AAMs. (BAE Systems)

Sea Harrier FRS.1 XZ493, delivered to No. 801 NAS in 1981, later served with the British Task Force during the Falklands Conflict. (Royal Navy)

RNAS Yeovilton was the designated Sea Harrier home base, with deliveries beginning in June 1979 to No. 899 Naval Air Squadron (NAS), the HQ unit. The first of the operational was No. 801 NAS, formed in March 1980 for the light aircraft carrier HMS *Invincible*, which was commissioned in July 1980, while No. 800 NAS was assigned to HMS *Illustrious*, launched in 1982.

A formation of three early production Sea Harrier: FRS.1s of No. 899 NAS in the foreground, No. 800 NAS in the centre, and No. 801 NAS. (Royal Navy)

Four BAe Sea Harrier FRS.1s of No. 800 NAS in the squadron's original colourful markings. (BAE Systems)

The compact design and anhedral wing is evident in the view of the Sea Harrier FRS.1 shipboard V/STOL multi-role fighter. (Francois Prins archive)

Early production Sea Harrier FRS.1s embarked on the commando carrier HMS *Bulwark* during carrier operation trials in the Atlantic in 1979. (Royal Navy)

A formation of No. 801 NAS Sea Harrier FRS.1s overflying HMS *Invincible* during an exercise in the Mediterranean Sea. (Royal Navy)

A No. 899 NAS Sea Harrier FRS.1 in its Falklands overall mid-grey colour scheme takes a bow at an airshow after operating in the South Atlantic. (David Oliver)

A follow-on batch of ten Sea Harrier FRS.1s was near completion when the Falklands Conflict began in April 1982 and twenty aircraft where dispatched, with the Task Force operating from *Invincible* and the helicopter carrier HMS *Hermes* fitted with a ski-jump. For their operations in the South Atlantic, the Sea Harriers were fitted with Tracor ALE-40 chaff/flare dispensers in the rear fuselage and 190-gallon drop tanks. Employed as fighter-bombers as well as interceptors, Sea Harriers destroyed at least twenty Argentine aircraft, including eight air-to-air kills, without loss, demonstrating outstanding serviceability in very severe conditions. None were lost in air combat but two fell to ground fire and four were lost in accidents. After the Falklands campaign, fourteen additional Sea Harriers were ordered plus another nine in September 1984.

Sea Harrier FRS.1 XZ450 was used extensively during trials with the ski-jump to assist take-off with a full weapons and fuel load. (BAE Systems)

A formation of Sea Harrier FRS.1s in their post-Falklands overall mid-grey colour scheme that became the standard for all the Royal Navy's aircraft. (Royal Navy)

A pair of No. 801 NAS BAe Sea Harrier FRS.1s with XZ498 in the foreground and XV490 armed with Sidewinder AAMs. (Royal Navy)

Sea Harrier FRS.1s of No. 801 NAS recover to the flight deck of the nuclear-powered aircraft carrier USS *Dwight D. Eisenhower* in 1984. (US Navy)

A Sea Harrier FRS.1 makes its take-off roll along the flight deck of the carrier HMS *Invincible* during NATO Exercise *Dragon Hammer* in 1990. (US Navy)

In 1985, BAe was awarded a contract for a mid-life update of the Royal Navy's Sea Harrier FRS.1. Two converted FRS.1s acted as prototypes, the first taking to the air on 19 September 1988, and in 1994 the upgraded aircraft was designated F/A.2. The most obvious external difference between the FRS.1 and F/A.2 was an enlarged radome housing the GEC-Marconi Blue Vixen pulse Doppler radar providing 'look-down shoot-down' capability and multiple target engagement. It also had a lengthened rear fuselage, a redesigned cockpit that included the relocation of weapon system controls to the up-front panel or the HOTAS control column, and duel multi-purpose HDDs to compliment the HUD. The F/A.2 had the ability of carrying four AIM-20 ARAAMs or ALARMs. The Pegasus 106 enabled short take-off air-to-surface attack sorties to be conducted with a weapons payload of up to 8,000 lb.

A pair of No. 801 NAS Sea Harrier F/A.2 fitted with air refuelling probes; inverted ZD610 was a converted FRS.1 while ZH812 was a new-build aircraft. (Crown Copyright)

A Sea Harrier F/A.2 of No. 801 Squadron fitted with an air-refuelling probe is seen in the hover as it recovers to HMS *Illustrious*. (Crown Copyright)

A No. 801 NAS Sea Harrier F/A.2 recovers to the flight deck of the amphibious assault ship HMS *Ocean* during Exercise *Saif Sareea II* off the coast of Oman in October 2001. (David Oliver)

Sea Harrier F/A.2s of No. 801 NAS on the flight deck of HMS *Invincible* while participating in Exercise *Aurora* off the coast of North Carolina in 2004. (Crown Copyright)

A Sea Harrier F/A.2 undergoing deep maintenance at BAE Warton, showing the open radome housing the Blue Vixen multi-mode radar. (BAE Systems)

Eighteen new-build F/A.2s were ordered and thirty-four FRS.1s were rotated through the upgrade programme between 1991 and 1994.

A small number of two-seat Harriers had been delivered to the Royal Navy, including three T.4Ns with Sea Harrier FRS.1 avionics but no radar, and five former RAF T.4s converted to T.8s for Sea Harrier F/A.2 lead-in trainers.

Left: A Royal Navy two-seat Harrier T.8N trainer in a dramatic vertical climb showing its lengthened rear reaction control pipe fairing to compensate for the longer nose. (Ian Black)

Right: Harrier T.8N ZD993, seen on approach to RNAS Yeovilton, was a converted T.4N equipped with Sea Harrier F/A.2 avionics. (Ian Black)

Left: Four No. 801 NAS F/A.2 Sea Harriers, based at RNAS Yeovilton, flying in formation in July 2005 led by ZH797, one of eighteen new-build aircraft. (Crown Copyright)

Right: Ten No. 801 NAS Harrier F/A.2s and two No. 3 Squadron RAF Harrier GR.7s belonging to Joint Force Harrier on the flight deck of HMS *Illustrious* in July 2002. (Royal Navy)

The Sea Harrier saw action in war again when it was deployed in the 1992–95 conflict in Bosnia, part of the Yugoslav Wars. F/A.2s launched raids on Serb forces and provided air-support for the international taskforce units conducting Operations *Deny Flight* and *Deliberate Force* against Bosnian Serb forces. On 16 April 1994, a Sea Harrier of No. 801 NAS, operating from the carrier HMS *Ark Royal*, was brought down by an Igla-1 surface-to-air missile fired by the Army of Republika Srpska while attempting to bomb Bosnian Serb tanks. The pilot, Lt Nick Richardson, ejected and landed in territory controlled by friendly Bosnian Muslims.

It was used again in the 1999 NATO campaign against the Federal Republic of Yugoslavia in Operation *Allied Force*; Sea Harriers that operated from HMS *Invincible* frequently patrolled the airspace to keep Yugoslav Air Force MiGs on the ground. They were also deployed to Sierra Leone on board HMS *Illustrious* in 2000, which was itself part of a Royal Navy convoy to supply and reinforce British intervention forces in the region.

Plans for the retirement of the Sea Harrier were announced in 2002 by the MoD. The aircraft's replacement, the Lockheed Martin F-35 Lightning II, was originally due in 2012 and the MoD argued that significant expenditure would be required to upgrade the fleet for only six years of service. The Sea Harrier was withdrawn from service in 2006, when the last remaining aircraft from No. 801 NAS were decommissioned on 29 March.

However, this was not the end of the Sea Harrier's service with the Royal Navy. Fourteen retired Sea Harriers were given a new lease of life as ground instruction aids for training flight deck personnel with the Royal Naval School of Flight Deck Operations (RNSFDO) based at RNAS Culdrose in Cornwall. Since the retirement of the last *Illustrious*-class carrier, HMS *Ark Royal* in 2010, RNSFDO has been training a new generation of fixed-wing aircraft handlers for the *Queen Elizabeth*-class aircraft carriers and their F-35 Lightning II aircraft. The RNSFDO Sea Harriers are able to taxi under their own power and although limiters have been fitted to restrict the aircraft to 50 per cent power, they can accelerate up to 25 kts to simulate a launch from the dummy deck at Culdrose. At the time of writing, the RNSFDO plans to keep the Sea Harrier F/A.2s operating from the dummy deck until 2020.

Sea Harrier F/A.2 ZH809 in the hover at an air display, painted in the original Sea Harrier FRS.1 colour scheme to celebrate twenty-five years of Royal Navy service in 2004. (Francois Prins)

This pristine No. 800 NAS Sea Harrier F/A.2, ZD607, a rebuilt FRS.1, is preserved at RAF Cottesmore. (David Oliver)

CHAPTER 4

'Corporate' Combat

On 2 April 1982 Argentine military forces invaded the British Falkland Islands, forcing the small British garrison of Royal Marines to surrender. Situated in the South Atlantic 480 miles north-east of Cape Horn, the Falklands had long been the subject of claims by Argentina, and the country's ruling Military Junta had decided to resolve the long-standing dispute with Britain over the Island's sovereignty by mounting a military takeover.

On 5 April the British government took the positive step of sending a strong Naval Task Force that included the aircraft carriers HMS *Hermes* and *Invincible*, with the intension of re-taking the Islands. Two days later Britain declared a 200-mile military Total Exclusion Zone (TEZ) around the Falklands and the same day the RAF flew the first operational sortie of Operation *Corporate*, when a Nimrod MR.1 undertook a surveillance mission from Ascension Island.

In order to mount an effective task force with which to re-take the Islands, it had to have a strong air component. To this end almost the entire Royal Navy Sea Harrier force – a total of twenty-eight aircraft – embarked on the two aircraft carriers, while frantic efforts were made to adapt a number of RAF Harrier GR.3s from No. 1(F) Squadron to operate alongside them in the South Atlantic. They were modified to take the RN 2-inch rockets that were compatible with the carrier's radar, Ferranti Inertial Navigation Reference and Attitude Equipment (FINRAE), and two Sidewinder AIM-9G AAMs. Bundles of chaff were carried in the airbrake recess and on 3 May three modified Harriers flew to Ascension Island on a record-breaking flight of 9 hours and 15 minutes.

RAF No. 1 (F) Squadron Harrier GR.3s refuelling from a Victor K.2 tanker en route to the Ascension Island on 4 May 1982. (RAF)

Two Harrier GR.3s armed with Sidewinder AAMs at Wideawake Airfield on Ascension Island with RAF Victor K.2 tankers and Nimrod MR.2s. (No. 1 Squadron archives)

Left: A Royal Navy Sea Harrier FRS.1, known during Operation *Corporate* as a SHAR, landing on the *Atlantic Conveyor* Ascension waters. (Royal Navy)

Right: Eight Royal Navy Sea Harrier FRS.1s and six RAF Harrier GR.3s loaded aboard the *Atlantic Conveyor* prior to its departure for the Falkland Islands on 8 May. (BAE Systems)

In the meantime the Sea Harriers, or SHARs as they were known in the Fleet Air Arm, had opened their combat score when nine attacked Stanley Airfield on the Falklands on the morning of 1 May, and following the sinking of the Argentine cruiser, *General Belgrano*, the first enemy aircraft, two Mirages and a Canberra, fell to the SHAR's Sidewinders.

A number of Sea Harrier pilots who took part in the Falklands Conflict were RAF officers serving with the Royal Navy on an exchange tour at the outbreak of hostilities. Flt-Lt Ted Ball was almost at the end of his two-year tour with No. 800 Naval Air Squadron when he was called from leave to join HMS *Hermes* that was about to lead the Task Force to the South Atlantic, and he subsequently flew sixty-nine sorties during Operation *Corporate*.

Having considerable experience of flying Harrier GR.3s with No. IV(AC) Squadron in RAFG, Flt-Lt Ball was to take part in a number of ground attack sorties in the Falkland Islands, including the first Sea Harrier raid of 1 May:

A total of nine SHARs were involved in the first attack on Stanley Airfield, some acting as cover while three laid CBUs on the runway and hangars. It was all over so quickly that there was no time for the intense AA-fire to register until we were returning to the carrier, when Flt Lt Dave Morgan felt his aircraft handling oddly and asked me to look over it. It had a large hole in the tailplane but he was able to land back on Hermes with no drama.

Combat Air Patrols (CAPs) were flown exactly as we had been trained to do, the only difference being the distance from the carrier was greater than during normal peacetime exercise so that out of a 1½-hour sortie, only 40 minutes was spent on station. Training and experience in Germany had prepared me for the ground attack mission, although not for seeing aircraft shot down during the raids. I took part in the second raid on Goose Green on 4 May with Lt Nick Taylor. I approached the target at high level before dropping to 80ft for the final run in. We had planned that I should arrive over the target slightly after Nick so that I would miss the blast from his 1,000-pounder. I began my run in at 500 kts and low as possible, I kept a watch out for where I knew Nick would be coming in. Almost as soon as I spotted him I saw a small explosion which was followed by a larger

A Sea Harrier FSR.1 of No. 801 NAS recovering to HMS *Invincible* to join another SHAR, which is chained down on the flight deck. (Neil Wookey)

A No. 809 NAS Sea Harrier FRS.1 armed with AIM-9L Sidewinder air-to-air missiles lands on HMS *Invincible*. (Royal Navy)

With the San Carlos forward operating base (FOB) blocked, and short of fuel, this SHAR had to divert to the assault ship HMS *Intrepid*. (Royal Navy)

Left: Harrier GR.3s of No. 1 (F) Squadron RAF with RN SHARs and a Sea King HAS.5 on HMS *Hermes*, the first GR.3 carrying a 1,000 lb GBU-16 Paveway II laser-guided bomb on its outer pylons. (IWM)

Right: A Sea Harrier FRS.1 begins its take-off run on HMS *Hermes* surrounded by two Harrier GR.3s and another SHAR. (BAE Systems)

The ground crew prepare a Harrier GR.3 on HMS *Hermes* for the Close Air Support (CAS) mission armed with Paveway II laser-guided LGBs. (IWM)

one, then his aircraft hit the ground and disintegrated in a ball of fire right in front of me. By the time I had taken my eyes off Nick's aircraft I was almost over the target and had to make some rapid adjustments in order to hit it. Most of the ground fire was now aimed at me but although it must have been pretty heavy, I was completely unaware of it at the time.

Despite its complexity, the Sea Harrier was easy to fly and proved to be remarkably robust and reliable, standing up very well to the hostile weather of the South Atlantic and capable of absorbing a considerable amount of ground fire damage which was more often than not patched up with aluminium tape. It was entirely predictable in operations and with the benefit of the improved cockpit layout the SHAR pilots had none of the head-down problems encountered in the Harriers.

Meanwhile, the modified RAF Harriers had flown to HMS *Hermes* via a merchant ship, the *Atlantic Conveyer*, which had taken them part of the way from Ascension Island. Although the Harrier had first landed on an aircraft carrier almost twenty years earlier, it was the first time for many of the RAF pilots in the South Atlantic. On 20 May they flew their first sorties in the Falklands, which were also the first time an RAF Harrier had fired in anger.

Left: Harrier GR.3s prepare to take-off from HMS *Hermes* for the first strike against Argentine troops on 20 May. (No. 1 Squadron archives)

Right: Equipped with Sidewinders, a SHAR takes off from the ski-jump on HMS *Hermes* with bombs and missiles on the flight deck. (Royal Navy)

A Harrier GR.3 armed with 1,000 lb iron bombs prepares to take off from the HMS *Hermes* flight deck, which is crowded with SHARs, Harriers and Sea King helicopters. (IWM)

Flt-Lt Tony Harper, one of twelve pilots from No. 1(F) Squadron to see action, flew a total of sixteen ground attack sorties during the conflict:

> My first operation was on 24 May when I was one of six Harriers that attacked Stanley just after dawn with 1,000 lb bombs, but one of the most satisfying raids was the one by three Harriers on Goose Green on 28 May in response to a request from 3 Para who were being pinned down by accurate enemy fire. Using detailed recce pictures taken by Harriers earlier in the day, we were able to pinpoint the enemy troop positions and hit them with CBUs and rockets so accurately that the vastly superior Argentine force surrendered to the Paras the following morning. I also flew another successful armed recce over enemy troops on Sapper Hill on 12 June, two days before the ceasefire.
>
> The Harrier was a very capable recce aircraft, but this ability was under-used in the Falklands. But it performed even better than we expected. It had the speed to avoid SAMs, was capable of taking considerable punishment from small arms fire, and the weather. However, the Sidewinders were never used and the FINRAE was useless before the landings. All navigation was dead-reckoning and as average transit distance between the Islands and the carriers was at least 200 miles, which was flown at 35,000 ft to conserve fuel, we always flew in pair with the leader navigating.

During the eight-week conflict, the twenty-eight Sea Harriers flew 1,453 operational sorties, shooting down thirty enemy aircraft plus three probable, while the Harriers flew a total of 126 sorties. While the Royal Navy Sea Harriers had been fully committed during Operation *Corporate*, it was felt that the RAF Harriers had not been used to the best advantage, especially after the British landings, and that they had lacked modern airfield denial weapons which would have considerably enhanced their ground attack capability.

RAF Harrier GR.3 move into Port Stanley Airfield following the surrender of the Argentine forces on 4 July 1982.

The Royal Navy SHAR detachment at Stanley Airfield servicing a Sea Harrier FRS.1 after the end of the Falklands Conflict. (Neil Wookey)

However, without the operational flexible, rugged Harrier and Sea Harrier with their unique ability to operate from aircraft carriers, short unprepared airstrips and helipads, the Falklands Islands, more than 8,000 miles from the British Isles, could not have been retaken.

HMS *Invincible* is welcomed back to Portsmouth on 17 September 1982 with No. 800 NAS Sea Harrier FRS.1s and No. 820 NAS Sea King helicopters on the flight deck. (Royal Navy)

Harrier GR.3 XW919 of No. 1 (F) Squadron was rebuilt after being hit by ground fire during the Falklands Conflict. (David Oliver)

After serving on HMS *Hermes* in the Falklands, No. 899 NAS SHAR ZA176 caused an international incident in June 1983 when Sub-Lt Ian Watson landed on a Spanish freighter after an avionics failure. It was converted to F/A.2 in 1995. (David Oliver)

CHAPTER 5

Defending the Colonies

Even before they hit the headlines in combat in the South Atlantic, RAF Harriers had been called on to protect a remote British colony many thousands of miles from the UK nearly five years earlier.

On the other side of the world a small British Colony in Central America had been the subject of threats from a neighbouring country for nearly a century. Belize, or British Honduras as it was called prior to June 1973 – a 9,000-square-mile strip of land along the western Caribbean Sea south of Mexico consisting mainly of jungle and swamp – is bordered on the west and south by Guatemala. First settled by British seamen in 1638, some of whom were thought to be Caribbean pirates seeking safe haven, rights of settlement along the Belize River were ceded to Britain by Spain in 1667. Both Mexico and Guatemala subsequently claimed to have inherited Spanish sovereignty over British Honduras, but Mexico recognised the existence of Belize in 1826 and Guatemala accepted a delimited frontier in 1859, but later claimed the agreement to be invalid.

The Guatemalan claim to the colony was revived in 1936, and after temporarily suspending it during the Second World War, raised it again in 1945.

A serious threat of invasion was made in February 1948, to which the British reacted by sending a Royal Navy cruiser, HMS *Sheffield*, and a battalion of the Gloucestershire Regiment to British Honduras. Although tension between the two countries persisted, there was no invasion, but in July 1960 Guatemalan forces moved back to the border areas in some strength. It was decided to send a detachment of RAF Shackleton MR.2 long-range maritime reconnaissance aircraft from Jamaica (where British troops had been deployed to quell internal unrest) to fly the flag over British Honduras.

The aircraft also flew a number of low-level patrols along the border with Guatemala in an effort to deter any thoughts of aggression from across the border. Later, the American consul in Guatemala staged through Stanley Field, informing the RAF aircrews that the Guatemalans had withdrawn their troops as soon as the 'Shacks' had appeared overhead.

Yet another threat of invasion was prompted by Britain's announcement that self-government would be introduced in the colony in the near future. By January 1972 there was yet another concentration of Guatemalan forces on the frontier, allegedly for an anti-guerrilla drive as the country was ravaged by a brutal civil war. This time Royal Navy Buccaneer S.2 low-level strike aircraft from No. 809 NAS, operating from the carrier HMS *Ark Royal*, then cruising in US waters off Florida, were despatched 'with haste' to 'show presence'. Two Buccaneers were launched along with two more acting as buddy tankers to make one of the longest ever flights of its type. The pair of Buccaneers overflew the British Honduras border with Guatemala before returning to the carrier – a six-hour, 2,600-mile round trip. This was enough to deter any further action by the Guatemalans.

Although RAF Harriers first came to public prominence during the Falklands Conflict, they were close to being used in action for the first time following one of Guatemala's periodical threats to invade the neighbouring British colony of Belize in November 1975, when six Harrier GR.1As of No. 1(F) Squadron were sent to Central America to reinforce the British Garrison via Goose Bay and Bermuda, supported by Victor tankers. Three Puma helicopters and an RAF Regiment squadron were also deployed.

However, in February 1976 Guatemala suffered a catastrophic earthquake, the hypocenter of which was located near the town of Los Amates, only 50 km south of Belize's southern border. With financial and military resources committed to disaster relief and reconstruction, Guatemala withdrew its forces from the border and in April 1976 the Harriers returned to the UK.

However, by June 1977 they had returned following yet more threats from Guatemala, whose superior air force included a squadron of A-37Bs and a number of T-33s. Belize, a country comprising mainly of jungle, swamp and mountains, with only one airport which had a short runway and few roads, was ideal Harrier country and following this latest threat it was decided to base a permanent detachment of Harrier GR.3s there. The high-profile role of the Harrier flight included low-level patrols within sight of the border, and although not fitted with Sidewinder AAMs, they carried out live weapons practice with their two 30 mm Aden cannon, Matra SNEB 68 mm unguided rockets, and 1,000 lb HE and cluster bombs, on the colony's isolated swamp ranges.

The flight was based at Stanley International Airport at Ladyville, with some 300 RAF personnel and being protected by four Rapier surface-to-air missile units. The Harriers operated from semi-permanent hides named using the NATO phonetic alphabet. *Alpha* and *Bravo* hides were set up in the grounds of the local brewery outside the gates to the garrison, while *Charlie* and *Delta* hides were set up on the other side of the garrison access road. *Foxtrot* and *Golf* hides were located around the airport fire station, with *Hotel*, *India* and *Juliet* hides arranged around the access taxiway and the edge of the airport apron.

After operating as a rotating roulement for two years, the Harrier detachment was put on an even more permanent footing with the formation of No. 1417 Flight from April 1980.

By the time Belize was granted full independence in September 1981, it was decided that the British garrison of some 1,500 troops and the RAF detachment for four Harrier GR.3s and four Puma HC.1 helicopters would be retained for 'an appropriate period'.

A No. 1417 (Tactical Ground Attack) Flight Harrier GR.Mk.3 prepares to leave its hide at Belize's Ladyville International Airport carrying SNEB rocket pods in September 1985. (David Oliver)

Harrier GR.3 'A', or *Alpha*, belonging to No. 1417 Flight, flying over Belize carrying a recce pod. (No. 1 (F) Squadron archives)

Three No. 1417 Flight Harrier GR.3s in *Alpha* hide, located next to the main gate of the Belize garrison. (David Oliver)

A No. 1417 Flight Harrier GR.3 in its hide under camouflage netting and with an umbrella over the cockpit acting as a sun shade. (David Oliver)

Charlie hide next to the main road into Belize City was one of six used by the No. 1417 Flight Harrier GR.3s in the 1980s. (David Oliver)

A Harrier GR.3 taxies out of its hide at Belize armed with SNEB unguided rockets and wearing the No. 1417 Flight's badge under the cockpit. (David Oliver)

No. 1417 Flight Harrier GR.3 'F' for Freddie taxies past a Rapier surface-to-air missile launcher unit used for airfield protection. (David Oliver)

Much flying was done, with plenty of flag-waving and sabre rattling, with the aircrew enjoying the posting due to the challenging missions and lack of restrictions. Eventually operations were confined to *Charlie/Delta* and *Foxtrot/Golf* hides, which went through a slow metamorphosis to permanent semi-hardened hides with concrete aprons and taxi-ways as well as block-built buildings that included accommodation, kitchen and bars.

The Harriers were drawn from Nos 1(F) and IV(AC) Squadrons and rotated every six months via Goose Bay, Canada and Bermuda. Three aircraft were lost while deployed to No. 1417 Flight: one was abandoned in December 1975 following a bird strike, another crashed into trees in May 1981 after failing to gain height during a vertical takeoff from Belize Airport, while the third struck trees near Georgeville only two months later. All three pilots ejected safely. Two more Harriers were severely damaged, one of which encountered a large vulture on approach to landing that tore straight into the intake, and the second due to a brownout while attempting to land on a short airstrip on St George's Caye, one of the many small islands off the coast of Belize.

The *Foxtrot/Golf* hide at Belize International Airport had a brick-built accommodation block for No. 1417 Flight personnel and a bar by 1990. (Petebutt)

A rarely seen four-ship formation of No. 1417 Flight Harrier GR.3s are difficult to spot against the canopy of the Belize jungle. (David Oliver)

Downtime for a No. 1417 Flight Harrier GR.3 in *Golf* hide, with an umbrella again being used to keep the sun off the open cockpit. (Petebutt)

Following the Argentine invasion of the Falkland Islands, serious consideration was given to use Belize as the main base for RAF operations in support of the UK task force sent to retake the islands. However, the size of its only airport mitigated against its use and the role fell to Wideawake Airfield on the mid-Atlantic Ascension Island.

It was not until 1991 that the Guatemalan government eventually recognised the self-determination of the Belizean people, ten years after its independence. This statement meant a significant alteration in Guatemala's foreign policy and it was followed in 1992 by a declaration of the Guatemalan president of the recognition of the independent state of Belize and the establishment of diplomatic relations between the two countries. Following this *de facto* declaration of peace, the Harriers, which were the last RAF GR.3s operated, were withdrawn from Belize in 1993.

By this time, the Harrier GR.5 had replaced the GR.3 in RAF service. Conceived as a joint venture by British Aerospace and McDonnell Douglas, the more powerful Harrier II could carry twice the weapon load of the GR.3 with a 50 per cent increase in its tactical radius. Although the GR.5 entered service with No. 233 OCU at RAF Wittering in May 1987, it was not considered combat ready when the UN-sanctioned Operation *Desert Storm* began in January 1991. The first Gulf War coincided with the first deliveries of the Harrier GR.7, an upgraded version with a day/night capability and the integration of 'smart' weapons. Service introduction was, however, plagued with teething problems that led to a period of grounding in 1991 and the effectiveness of a dedicated STOVL combat aircraft to be called into question. The Harrier made one last deployment to Belize in September 1993, when Harrier GR.7s of No. IV(AC) Squadron flew to the former colony via Goose Bay in Canada, and Key West in Florida, air-refueled by VC.10 tankers. This was a 'flag-waving' exercise to demonstrate the RAF's ability to deter potential aggressors at short notice.

However, more than twenty years after the last RAF Harrier flew out of Belize, Guatemala was still claiming a large swath of Belize's territory and the issue was referred to the International Court of Justice.

No. IV (AC) Squadron Harrier GR.7s took part in the last RAF deployment to Belize in 1993, flying via Goose Green, Canada, and Key West in Florida. (BAE Systems)

CHAPTER 6

Last Action Heroes

Evolved from a joint design study by British Aerospace and McDonnell Douglas to meet Air Staff Requirement (ASR) 407, the GR Mk.5 was developed to enable the Harrier concept to remain viable in the 1990s. Powered by 21,750 lb thrust Pegasus 105 turbofan, the GR.5 featured the new enlarged supercritical carbon fibre composite wing with LERX, developed for the AV-8B, which first flew in November 1978. However, it was not until 1981 that the RAF placed an order for sixty GR.5s, the first of which flew at Dunsfold on 30 April 1985.

The single-piece wing and front fuselage were built in the United States by McDonnell Douglas, with British Aerospace building the aft and centre fuselage and tail and assembling the aircraft at Dunsfold.

The avionics were entirely new, with an advanced Zeus ECM system in the rear tail fairing and the Hughes ARBS. It was armed with the newly developed twin 25 mm Aden cannon and AIM-9L Sidewinder AAMs, plus 9,2200 lb of weapons on seven under-wing pylons.

The main role of the GR.5 was battlefield support of RAFG, and the first unit equipped was No. 3 Squadron at RAF Wildenrath in March 1989. A total of forty-three GR.5s and nineteen upgraded GR.5As were delivered to the RAF.

However, during the build up to Operation *Desert Storm* in 1990–91, the RAF Harrier GR.5 were not considered combat ready and an updated variant was already under development. From November 1989, fifty-nine GR.5 were being upgraded to night-capable GR.7s, which featured forward-looking infra-red (FLIR), Nightbird night vision goggles (NVG), digital colour moving-map display to assist target acquisition and wide-angle HUD/HDD. A Vincen reconnaissance pod was carried off the centerline pylon using infra-red line-scan, panoramic and long-range oblique cameras. They were followed by thirty-four new-build aircraft delivered between May 1990 and June 1992. Armed with the twin 25 mm Aden cannon, the GR.7's eight under-wing pylons could carry a maximum of 13,325 lb of weapons, including Paveway laser-guided bombs (LGB), BL755 cluster bombs, 68 mm unguided rockets and AIM-9 Sidewinders.

Service introduction was plagued with teething troubles with its electrical system and the 25 mm gun installation. No. 3 Squadron in RAFG received its first GR.7s in November 1990, followed by No. 1(F) Squadron and No. 20(Reserve) Squadrons at RAF Wittering in November 1992 and January 1993 respectively.

In April 1993, Harrier GR.7s replaced RAF Jaguars supporting Operation *Warden*, a United Nations operation to defend Kurds in Northern Iraq, and in December 1994 they again took over the former Jaguar role in Operation *Grapple*, in support of the UN peacekeeping missions in the former Yugoslavia.

During the lead up to the second Gulf War, the British deployment of support to Operation *Telic* included Harrier GR.7s of Nos 1(F), 3 and IV(AC) Squadrons, based at Al Jaber in Kuwait, in March and April 2003. Equipped with the BAE Systems Thermal Imaging Airborne Laser Designator (TIALD), the RAF Harriers flew a total of 430 offensive sorties dropping RBL755 CBUs, Paveway III LGBs, and, for the first time, AGM-65G2 Maverick air-to-ground missiles.

Despite these limited deployments, for nearly a decade following the end of the Cold War the RAF Harrier's star had been waning, but its fortune was to be revived as a result of events on 11 September 2001. On that day, a suicide attack by Al Qaeda terrorists on New York killed more than 3,000 people and set in motion a war on the other side of the globe.

On 7 October 2001, US and British forces launched Operation *Enduring Freedom*, with aerial bombing campaigns in Afghanistan targeting Taliban and Al Qaeda training camps, prior to a NATO-mandated invasion of Afghanistan by ground troops. After the fall of Kabul in November, the number of British forces in Afghanistan increased dramatically to support a US-led coalition fighting a resurgent Taliban.

Herrick was the operational name under which all British operations in the war in Afghanistan were conducted since 2002. It comprised the British contribution to the NATO-led International Security Assistance Force (ISAF) and support to the US-led Operation *Enduring Freedom*. Since NATO took command of ISAF in 2003, Operation *Herrick* increased in size and strength to match the growing geographical intervention in Afghanistan.

Left: At Al Jaber Air Base in Kuwait, RAF ground crew pre-flight an RAF Harrier GR.7 assigned to Operation *Telic*, the British deployment to support coalition forces attacking Iraq in April 2003. (Crown Copyright)

Right: An RAF pilot climbs aboard a Harrier GR.7 based at Al Jaber Air Base in Kuwait for an Operation *Telic* strike sortie against Iraqi forces. (Crown Copyright)

Armed with 540 lb GP bombs and Sidewinder AAMs, a Harrier GR.7 taxies out at Al Jaber Air Base for an Operation *Telic* sortie. (Crown Copyright)

Lined up to take off at Al Jaber Air Base in April 2003 is an RAF Harrier GR.7 armed with four RBL755 Cluster Bomb Units (CBU). (Crown Copyright)

A No. 1 (Fighter) Squadron Harrier GR.7 on an Operation *Herrick* patrol over the Afghan mountains in 2005 armed with a Paveway II and a 540 lb GP bomb on the inner pylons, a Terma Advanced Infra-Red Countermeasures (AIRCM) pod and a Saab BOL self-defence pod on the mid-pylons. (No. 1 Squadron archives)

Close encounters to No. 1(F) Squadron Harrier GR.7A ZD348, armed with CRV-7 rocket pods and assigned to Operation *Herrick*, patrolling Helmand Province in February 2006. (No. 1 Squadron archives)

In response to a coalition request for the United Kingdom to provide a Close Air Support (CAS) capability to coalition forces operating in Southern Afghanistan, the UK MoD agreed to deploy six RAF Harrier GR.7s in September 2004. The aircraft were initially provided by No. 3 Squadron and were flown by No. 1(F) Squadron crews for what was planned to be only a nine-month deployment. For the first time since its formation three years earlier, Joint Force Harrier (JFH) was about to show its teeth.

Although USAF units operated from the vast former Soviet air base at Bagram, and NATO coalition air forces from Kabul, the closest airfield to the British area of operations in Helmand Province was Kandahar Airfield (KAF). Built in 1962 with US financial aid and technical assistance under the US International Development Program, Kandahar Airport was intended to become the largest international airport in Central Asia. However, it was severely damaged by Soviet air attacks between 1979 and 1989, and US air raids during the opening days of Operation *Enduring Freedom*, when the airport was the site of what was thought at the time to be the Taliban's 'last stand'.

Flares are fired from a heavily armed No. 1(F) Squadron Harrier GR.7 on a medium altitude patrol over Helmand Province in February 2006. (No. 1 Squadron archives)

Harrier GR.7A ZD433 taxies out to Kandahar Airfield's damaged runway armed with a 540 lb general-purpose bomb on the outer pylon and a CRV-7 six-rocket pod on the mid-pylon in April 2006. (David Oliver)

RAF ground crews prepare a Harrier GR.9 under its sunshade, armed with Paveway II LGBs on the inner pylons and equipped with a TIALD pod, at Kandahar Airfield (KAF) during Operation *Herrick* in November 2006. (David Oliver)

An RAF pilot with his 'g'-suit and life-preserver over his tropical flying suit climbs aboard his Harrier GR.7 in a soft-skin aircraft shelter at Kandahar Airfield (KAF) in November 2006. (David Oliver)

Harrier GR.9 ZD347 wearing bomb mission symbols taxies out of its shelter at KAF armed with GBU-12 Paveway II LGBs and equipped with a TIALD pod. (David Oliver)

By the time British combat aircraft were deployed to Afghanistan, KAF's 10,000 ft runway was breaking up and in serious need of repair. The only type that could use it safely in the high summer temperatures with a full weapons payload was the RAF Harrier with its short field take-off and landing capability. Early operations involved nothing more than scaring away the enemy with a 'show of force' – flying at 100 ft at full throttle firing off chaff and flares. However, the tempo rose when British troops went on the offensive in Helmand Province in early 2006.

Over 500 540 lb and 1,000 lb 'iron' bombs were dropped by No. IV(AC) Squadron between May and October 2006 during its second deployment in the country. The Harrier's mission was Close Air Support (CAS), tactical reconnaissance and low and high tempo war fighting, often flying in 'packages' with USAF A-10s and B-52s. Up to August 2006, mainly day missions had been flown, but 24-hour availability became necessary as the ground fighting intensified and the number of Harriers was increased to seven as operational flying hours doubled to some 480 a month.

No. IV(AC) Squadron Harrier GR.7A ZD347 taxies to the KAF runway threshold carrying drop tanks on the outer pylons and Paveway II LGBs on the inner pylons. (David Oliver)

Former No. 20 Squadron Harrier GR.7A ZD433 on the perimeter track at KAF loaded with outer pylon drop tanks, inner pylon Paveway II LGBs and an underbelly Sniper Advanced Targeting Pod. (David Oliver)

The mission marking carried by Harrier GR.7A ZD433 include, from left to right, twenty-three CRV-7 2.75 inch rocket firing missions with six and nineteen rocket pods, and six 540 lb GP bombs with air burst and six with impact fusing. (David Oliver)

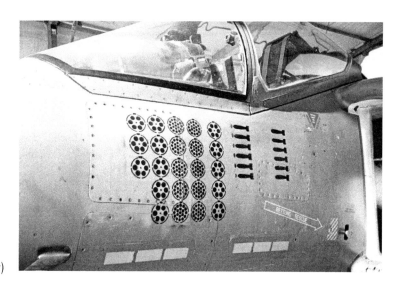

With the Helmand hills in the background, No. 1 (F) Squadron Harrier GR.7 ZD433 taxies to Kandahar Airfield's single damaged runway in December 2006 with its airbrake extended. (David Oliver)

Harrier GR.7A ZD404 taxies out to begin a Close Air Support mission from Kandahar Airfield in April 2006 with *Lucy* nose art along with three 540 lb GP bomb and nineteen precision guided munition (PMG) mission markings. (David Oliver)

When No. 800 NAS took over in September 2006 under the command of its charismatic CO, Commander Adrian Orchard RN, triple trade maintainers introduced their own flexi-maintenance package, which reduced the down-time of the Harriers in their charge. Commander Orchard likened Operation *Herrick* to a Korea-type war and said that it was, 'The most mentally challenging flying I have done.'

In order to self-designate targets, the GR.7s initially used the BAE systems' TIALD pod equipped with a high resolution Forward-Looking Infra-Red (FLIR) and a laser designator that automatically tracks the target once it has locked on. However, Operation *Herrick* highlighted the shortfalls of the TIALD pod, especially in the urban CAS role. As a result an Urgent Operational Requirement (UOR) was issued in late 2006 for a new pod, resulting in the first AN/AAQ-33 Sniper Advanced Targeting Pod being test-flown on a Harrier GR.9 in December 2006. A contract was awarded to Lockheed Martin in February 2007, and deliveries of the pods were completed only four months later. Sniper allowed the Harrier pilot to detect and identify weapons caches, and even individuals carrying arms, while the aircraft was far enough away for it not to be heard. In early May 2007, No. IV(AC) Squadron became the first RAF unit to train with Sniper, taking it with them when the squadron deployed to Afghanistan again in mid-June 2007. When linked with the handheld L3 Remote Operations Video Enhanced Receiver (Rover) terminal, joint forward air controllers (JFAC) on the ground could view real-time imagery downloaded from the Harrier's targeting pod.

The Harriers were armed with a mix and weapons and recce/targeting pods also used Paveway IIs and Enhanced Paveway (EPW) II and III plus laser-guided munitions, 'iron' bombs, AGM-65G-2 Maverick day/night air-to-surface missiles, CRV-7 unguided rockets and AIM-9L sidewinders, for self-defence. What many pilots regretted was summed up by Royal Marine Major Dave Kelly, a former Sea Harrier pilot serving with No. 1(F) Squadron that was deployed to Afghanistan from December 2005 to May 2006. Simply put it was: 'No guns! – Pity.' Although the twin 25 mm Aden gun installation problems had been overcome, it was never part of the GR.9's *Herrick* weapons fit.

However, the Harrier GR.9 was the lead airframe for the Global Positioning System Aided Inertial Navigation System (GAINS)/laser-guided Paveway IV, and for anti-armour and high-value battlefield targets the MBDA Brimstone Missile was later adopted. In addition to CAS, the Harriers undertook non-traditional intelligence, surveillance and reconnaissance (ISR) in Afghanistan to determine enemy activity and provide that information to troops on the ground. Up to eleven Harriers were deployed at Kandahar at any one time, and the force begun to transition to upgraded GR.9As towards the end of 2007.

A good luck message from *Lucy* for the Harrier pilots deployed to Operation *Herrick* in 2006 adorned the nose of Harrier GR.7A ZD404. (David Oliver)

Between the CRV-7 and 540 lb GP bomb mission markings worn by Harrier GR.9 ZD437, *Michelle's* message to its pilot is 'Enjoy the Ride!!!' (David Oliver)

No. 800 NAS GR.7 ZG471 breaks cover from its soft-skin hangar into the setting sun at KAF, armed with GP bombs on the outer pylons, six CRV-7 rocket pods on the mid-pylons and an underbelly Sniper ATP. (David Oliver)

In November 2006 Harrier GR.7 ZG471 had conducted two PGM, six CRV-7 rocket, two 540 lb GP bomb with impact fusing and two 540 lb GP bomb with air burst fusing missions. (David Oliver)

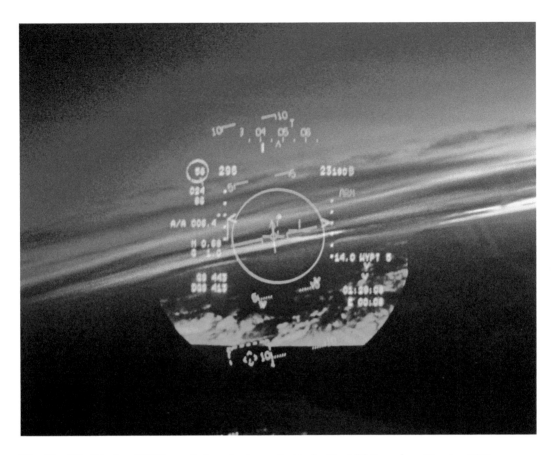

The Head-Up-Display (HUD) symbology in the cockpit of a No. 1(F) Squadron Harrier GR.7 on a night mission over Helmand Province in Afghanistan. (No. 1 Squadron archives)

In early 2008, the Harrier fleet began a mid-life upgrade that saw the GR.7s modified as GR.7As, GR.9s or GR.9As. The GR.7A had a Rolls-Royce Pegasus Mk.107 power plant in place of the GR.7's Mk.105, adding 3,000 lb of thrust. A total of forty such modifications were made. In addition, around seventy GR.7 and GR.7As benefited from an avionics and weapons upgrade to become GR.9s, which became the new baseline standard for the Harrier fleet. GR.7As that had gone through both the avionics and engine upgrades were designated GR.9As.

JFH was also responsible for providing combat aircraft for the Royal Navy's aircraft carriers and along with the Operation *Herrick* commitment, this meant that JFH was among the RAF's most frequently deployed assets. In March 2007 the Naval Strike Wing (NSW) was formed, comprising elements of No. 800 and No. 801 NAS to form what was the Fleet Air Arm's only fixed-wing strike force.

However, by this time the MoD had decided to replace the Harriers in Afghanistan with Tornado GR.4 aircraft, and No. 1(F) Squadron brought its eight Harrier GR.9As back from KAF to RAF Cottesmore for the last time in July 2010.

Harriers had completed an uninterrupted five-year deployment in theatre – the longest period of high-tempo sustained operations since the Second World War. During this time the RAF's Harrier proved itself extremely reliable and effective, with JFH accomplishing 8,557 operational sorties, 22,772 flying hours and a remarkable technical serviceability rate of more than 99 per cent. None were lost to enemy fire or accident, and only one was severely damaged enough to be air freighted back to the UK (after being hit on the ground at KAF during a rocket attack in 2005).

Blast pen artwork at Kandahar Airfield from the first two Harrier deployments to Operation *Herrick* of Nos IV(AC) and 1(F) Squadrons in Afghanistan. (David Oliver)

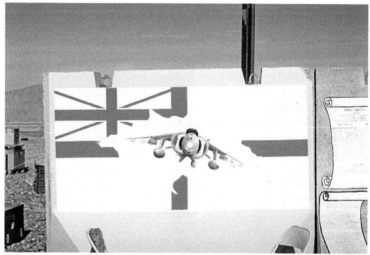

Unfinished blast pen artwork by No. 800 Naval Air Squadron ground crew at Kandahar Airfield in 2006. (David Oliver)

A Harrier GR.9 ZG477 from No. IV (AC) Squadron, RAF Cottesmore, during a sortie over Afghanistan in November 2008 from KAF armed with Paveway IV laser-guided bombs. (Crown Copyright)

Above: Harrier GR.9 ZG511, based at KAF, during a CAS mission over Helmand Province as part of Operation *Herrick* in December 2008, carrying Paveway IVs on the outer pylons, CRV-7 pods on the mid-pylons, drop tanks on the inner pylons and a Digital Joint Recce Pod (DJRP) and a Sniper ATP under the belly. (USAF)

Below: No. 1(F) Squadron Harrier GR.9 ZG505 Squadron takes off from Kandahar Airfield to return home in June 2009 after a five-year deployment in Afghanistan. (Crown Copyright)

CHAPTER 7

Flying Leathernecks

Since its inception in 1957, the P1127/Kestrel series of V/STOL aircraft and its revolutionary Pegasus engine had received strong support from the United States. Although the US Marine Corps had not taken part in the Tripartite trials, the arrival of the six XV-6As in the United States in 1966 allowed Marine pilots to fly the aircraft. Although the US Air Force and Navy saw the XV-6A trials simply as academic exercises, the Marines were impressed by the aircraft's simplicity and flexibility. Despite this, it was with the development of the Harrier that their interest was rekindled, and in early 1969 a US Navy team visited Dunsfold to carry out a detailed assessment of the aircraft. Although it was through the US Navy that the Marines purchased their aircraft, making the second evaluation necessary, it was also vital to gain support in Congress for the purchase of this foreign aircraft. If the majority of aircraft could be manufactured under licence in the United States by McDonnell Douglas, the Marines were allowed to order an initial twelve Harrier Mk.50s, equivalent to the RAF GR.3, for delivery from Hawker Siddeley – the aircraft initially being allocated the service designation of AV-6B, which was soon changed to AV-8A.

The US Marine Corps ordered a total of 102 AV-8As, the first of which was delivered on 26 January 1971, followed by eight two-seat TAV-8As. A number of AV-8As were later converted to AV-8C standard, which involved the installation of ECM equipment and adding a new inertial navigation system to the aircraft's avionics, and substantial changes included Lift Improvement Devices to increase VSTOL performance.

A Sidewinder AAM armed Hawker Siddeley AV-8A in the hover belonging to VMA-513, the first US Marine Corps Attack Squadron to operate the type in 1971. (USMC)

A pair of Kingston-built Harrier Mk.50, designated AV-8As, assigned to VMA-231 that operated from aircraft carrier USS *Franklin D. Roosevelt.* (USMC)

Two of the 102 AV-8A Harrier aircraft delivered to the US Marine Corps, which were assigned to VMFA-513 in 1975. (USMC)

In 1975, McDonnell Douglas decided to proceed with an improved version of the BAe Harrier, having acquired production and development rights for the aircraft as part of the agreement under which the AV-8As were purchased by the USMC. Supported by the USMC, the first of two McDonnell Douglas YAV-8B aerodynamic prototypes, both converted from AV-8As, flew for the first time in St Louis on 9 November 1978. Work proceeded at the beginning of 1981 on four Full-Scale Development (FSD) Harrier IIs, the first of which flew in 1981, and the first USMC Harrier II was delivered to US Marine Corps Air Station (MCAS) Cherry Point in December 1983.

With an entirely new super-critical section wing, the main box of which was produced entirely in carbon fibre composite with slotted training-edge flaps and leading-edge root extensions (LERX), an airframe constructed of 25 per cent carbon fibre, a 21,180 lb thrust Rolls-Royce F402 vectored-thrust turbofan engine with improved front nozzles and a raised cockpit to improve the pilot's view, the AV-8B Harrier II could carry twice the weapon load of the Harrier GR.3 on six under-wing pylons. The USMC AV-8B was equipped with an advanced internal Electronic Countermeasures (ECM) system, the Hughes Angle/Rate Bombing System (ARBS).

Production of the Harrier II began at St Louis in 1981, and a total of 337 AV-8Bs were acquired for the USMC, including twenty-eight two-seat TAV-8Bs that entered service with VMAT-203 at Cherry Point, North Carolina, in late 1987.

A VMA-513 AV-8A
Harrier aircraft, armed
with twin cannon pods
and fitted with an
air refuelling probe,
taking off from the
amphibious assault
ship USS *Nassau* in
1982. (US Navy)

A retired two-seat
USMC TAV-8A (eight of
which were delivered
in 1976) used to train
fire-fighting crews on
board the amphibious
assault carrier
USS *Essex* in 2017.
(US Navy)

The first prototype
McDonnell Douglas
YAV-8B Harrier II
after its roll-out and
before its first flight
on 9 November 1978.
(McDonnell Douglas)

The prototype YAV-8B was an AV-8A that was modified with the new large wing and uprated Pegasus 11 F402-RR-404 turbofan. It is seen carrying Sidewinder AAMs. (McDonnell Douglas)

The second Full-Scale Development (FSD) AV-8B, which introduced wing leading-edge root extensions, first flew in April 1982. (BAE Systems)

An early production McDonnell Douglas AV-18B Harrier II at the hover with markings of the USA, Italy and Spain, who had ordered the type. (McDonnell Douglas)

An USMC AV-8B wearing the early two-tone grey/green camouflage scheme in the hover, showing its six under-wing pylons. (USMC)

A trio of early night-attack-capable AV-8Bs recover to the flight deck of the amphibious assault ship USS *Tarawa* in 2002. (US Navy)

In 1991, Harrier IIs were the first US Marine Corps tactical aircraft to arrive for Operation *Desert Storm* over the Persian Gulf. Some thirty-five USMC AV-8Bs, operating from King Abdul Aziz Air Base in Saudi Arabia, provided air support to coalition ground forces during the 100-hour land battle attacking Iraqi armoured vehicles and troop concentrations for the loss of only two aircraft. During the forty-two days of combat, eighty-six AV-8B Harrier IIs flew 3,380 combat sorties and dropped a higher weight of ordnance than any type other than the B-52, for the loss of five aircraft and two pilots from surface-to-air missiles. In 1999 USMC AV-8Bs participated in the NATO bombing campaign of Yugoslavia during Operation *Allied Force* and the 2003 Iraq War, flying more than 2,000 sorties in the close support role.

Production of all versions of the AV-8B at St Louis ended in 2003 with delivery of the last Harrier II, by which time McDonnell Douglas had merged with Boeing.

In June 2007, the US Department of Defense awarded a $258.5 million performance-based logistics contract to the Boeing Company for the AV-8B Harriers operated by USMC, Italy and Spain under the Harrier Integrated Supply Support (HISS) programme, which resulted in the development of the AV-8B Plus. Powered by a 2,340 lb thrust Rolls-Royce Pegasus F402-RR-408, the AV-8B Plus cockpit is fully integrated for day and night operations and is equipped with head-up and head-down displays, a digital moving map, an inertial navigation system (INS) and a HOTAS.

Thirsty USMC AV-8B Plus Harrier IIs with Litening targeting pods on the starboard inner pylon approach a USAF KC-10 tanker during Operation *Iraqi Freedom* in 2004. (USAF)

A pair of yellow tail VMA-542 'Tigers' night-capable AV-8Bs with the FLIR fitted in the small fairing above the nose. (BAE Systems)

A VMA-231 'Ace of Spades' AV-8B Plus at the Camp Dywer fuel pits in Afghanistan in 2010, with an AN/AAQ-28(V)4 Litening sensor pod on the starboard under-wing pylon. (US Navy)

The Harrier II Plus can be armed with a wide range of weapon systems, including the AIM-120A AMRAAM and Sparrow missiles, AGM-65 Maverick air-to-surface missiles, anti-ship Harpoon and MBDA Sea Eagle missiles, a 25 mm cannon and a range of bombs and rockets. The Maverick AGM-65 anti-tank missile is installed on the Italian Harrier II Plus.

AV-8B aircraft have been fitted with the Northrop Grumman Litening II targeting and reconnaissance pod. Litening II consists of a CCD TV camera for video reconnaissance and FLIR and laser spot tracker or rangefinder for targeting. It is fitted with the APG-65 radar that provides high-resolution, long-range surface mapping and detection, and tracking of land-based and sea-based targets.

USMC AV-8Bs have been involved in operations over Afghanistan since 7 October 2001, when Operation *Enduring Freedom* began with US and British forces conducting airstrikes on Taliban and Al Qaeda targets in Afghanistan. However, is was over a decade later that US Marine Corps lost no less than six AV-8Bs in one night, a result of a disastrous attack by Taliban insurgents. On the evening of 13 September 2013, a group of fifteen attackers cut their way into Camp Bastion (which was considered to be an impregnable fortress) to destroy aircraft and kill US marines sleeping in their tents in the US complex known as Camp Leatherneck.

One of their objectives was the destruction of Marine Attack Squadron 211 (VMA-211) AV-8B Harrier IIs being worked in temporary hangars only 500 ft from the perimeter fence, and although the alarm was raised at 22.00 hours, they succeeded.

After a two-hour fire-fight with Marines, RAF Regiment gunners and Apache and Super Cobra helicopters, fourteen of the attackers were dead and one was captured. However, during the battle two US personnel had been killed, including VMA-211's commanding officer Lt-Col Christopher Raible, and eight wounded, along with several RAF personnel. The attackers also succeeded in destroying six AV-8Bs and severely damaged two more. It was the US Marine Corps' worst loss of aircraft in a single incident since the Vietnam War.

On 27 July 2014, the amphibious assault ship USS *Bataan* began deploying USMC AV-8Bs over Iraq to provide surveillance of the so-called Islamic State of Iraq and the Levant (ISIL) forces. Surveillance operations continued as part of Operation *Inherent Resolve* against ISIL militants and in early September 2014 AV-8Bs attacked an ISIL target in Iraq, marking the first time a USMC unit dropped ordnance in the operation. USMC AV-8B operations continued in 2016 from USS *Boxer*, the flagship for the Boxer Amphibious Ready Group, with the embarked 13th Marine Expeditionary Unit (MEU).

A USMC Harrier II receives fuel over the rugged mountain terrain of Afghanistan's Helmand Province from a USAF KC-10 Extender in 2012, with a good view of the AV-8B Plus nose-mounted FLIR and the pilot's wide-angle HUD. (USAF)

VMA-211 'Wake Island Avengers' AV-8B Plus launches at Camp Bastion, Helmand Province, Afghanistan, in September 2012 where, exactly a year later, the USMC suffered its worst loss since the Vietnam War when the Taliban destroyed six VMA-211 AV-8B aircraft. (US Navy)

An AV-8B Harrier assigned to Air Test and Evaluation Squadron VX-31 'Dust Devils' conducts the first test flight of a mix of 50-50 jet fuel and biofuel over the Naval Air Warfare Center Weapons Division, China Lake. (US Navy)

An AV-8B Harrier assigned to the 'Black Sheep' of VMA-214 prepares for take-off as another lands aboard the amphibious assault ship USS *Makin Island*. (US Navy)

One of two VMA-542 'Tigers' AV-8B Plus Harrier IIs flying in a low level formation breaks away. Note the pilot's wide-angle HUB in the cockpit of the aircraft in the foreground. (Francois Prins archive)

A VMA-513 'Flying Nightmares' AV-8B Harrier accelerates along the flight deck of the amphibious assault ship USS *Bataan* in the Atlantic Ocean. (US Navy)

The long nose radome of this AV-8B Plus Harrier II taking off from the amphibious assault ship USS *Bataan* houses its APG-pulse Doppler multi-mode radar. (US Navy)

On 1 August 2016, USMC Harriers from USS *Wasp* began strikes against ISIL as part of manned and unmanned airstrikes on targets near Sirte, launching at least five times within two days.

For more than thirty years, the McDonnell Douglas/Boeing AV-8B Harrier II has been the USMC's primary fixed-wing Close Air Support (CAS) platform. It is the only combat aircraft to be designed to operate amphibious assault ships and austere expeditionary airfields in support of Marine Expeditionary Units (MEU).

In 2017, the USMC had an active fleet of 112 AV-8B Harriers, which were due for retirement in 2026. Stationed at MCAS Yuma in Arizona is Marine Aircraft Group (MAG)-13, the West Cost Harrier centre with three VMAs. MAG-14 at MCAS Cherry Point, North Carolina is the home base of three Harrier-equipped VMAs and Marine Attack Training Squadron (VMAT)-203 with the two-seat TAV-8B. There is also a VMA Harrier detachment at MCAS Iwakuni in Japan.

VMAT-203, based at Cherry Point, is responsible for training new Harrier pilots. Trainee pilots begin with two weeks of ground school followed by thirteen simulator 'flights'. After some ten flights with the Instructor Pilot (IP) in the TAV-8B, students will fly solo in a single-seat AV-8B.

While the aircraft is relatively easy to fly, its multiple types of landing and take-off modes are the challenge for the Harrier's student pilots. Conventional, fixed-nozzle, variable-nozzle, rolling vertical and vertical have to be perfected, while student pilots have to complete thirty-six Field Carrier Landing Practice (FCLP) landings (carried out at Brogue Field near Cherry Point) and carry out Forward-Based Operations (FBO) by doing slow landings into a short airfield.

The six-month syllabus also consists of formation and night flights before they embark on the tactical phase of the training, comprising air-to-ground, basic air-to-air, CAS and threat reaction. For advanced weapons training, including the employment of air-to-ground ordnance, student pilots join a VMAT-203 detachment at MCAS Yuma in Arizona for a six-week course. Using the nearby Chocolate Mountain Aerial Gunnery Range, the training involves day and night missions employing live Mk.82 fin-retarded 500 lb Snakeye bombs, GBU-54 laser Joint Direct Attack Munition (JDAM), 5-inch Zuni rockets and cluster munitions, as well as firing the GAU-12 five-barrel 25 mm cannon.

Equipped with the latest advanced precision weapons and the Northrop Grumman AN/AAQ-28 Litening targeting pod with streaming video downlinks, and beyond-visual-range (BVR) air-to-air radar missiles, the AV-8B flies vital and currently irreplaceable missions with the Marine Air-to-Ground Task Force (MAGTF)

The STOVL tactical aircraft has been in continual use since Operation *Desert Storm* to Operation *Odyssey Dawn* in Libya, Operation *Enduring Freedom* in Afghanistan and the current Operation *Inherent Resolve* in Iraq and Syria.

Marines transport GBU-54 bombs on the flight deck of amphibious assault ship USS *Makin Island* for loading on a VMA-221 AV-8B Plus during Operation *Inherent Resolve* against ISIL forces. (US Navy)

USMC currently maintains five active operational VMAs, each with sixteen aircraft, which it plans to maintain until 2020, while MAG-13 will convert to F-35B Joint Strike Fighters by 2022 and MAG-14 by 2026.

However, USMC is facing a challenge to keep its venerable fleet operational. As of July 2013, approximately 110 aircraft have been damaged beyond repair since the type entered service in 1985.

By 2017 the AV-8B faced increasingly serious shortfalls in spares, a problem that is being addressed through the Harrier Independent Readiness Review (HIRR), which focuses on major components that are likely to fail or require replacement. The HIRR highlighted three key areas of concern, improvements needed in maintenance – which include maintenance timeline management and moving the supply system away from Boeing to the US Navy – manpower and material shortage. As a readiness goal, the Marine Corps established a total of fifty-five Ready Basic Aircraft (RBA) in the operational squadrons while ensuring known deficiencies were addressed, especially those relating to the F402 Pegasus engine, and that programme-related engineering was kept at acceptable levels.

The USMC has also made plans to make improvements to the aircraft. In 2015 the AV-8B fleet received the H6.1 operational Flight Program (OFP) to integrate the Generation 4 Litening targeting pod and correct software deficiencies in smart weapon employment and carriage. Airborne Variable Message Format (VMF) terminals were installed, enabling the AV-18B to accept joint standard Digital-Aided Close Air Support (DCAS) technology.

The digital video recorder and the BRU-70/A Digital Improved Triple Ejector Rack (DITER) were also integrated and the carriage of the AIM-120 was expanded. At the same time the Deployable Mission Rehearsal Trainer (DMRT) that enables deployed forces to continue training and retraining proficiency with the aircraft's advanced systems was introduced.

The fielding of the H6.2 OFP, which will integrate Link 16 Positive Position Location and Identification (PPLI) capability, is planned for 2018, with FAA-compliant required navigation performance/area navigation capability that will correct other software deficiencies identified during recent combat operations. In addition, the USMC plans to incorporate OFP H7.0 that will provide full Link 16 integration into all AV-8B II Plus radar-equipped aircraft and the installation of a further IFP upgrade to enable the AV-8B to be digitally interoperable with future network infrastructure.

On 29 June 2016, VMFA-211 'Wake Island Avengers' became the first AV-8B operational squadron to transition to the Lockheed Martin F-35B, the STOVL variant of the Lockheed Martin Lightning II.

A VMA-311 'Tomcats' AV-8B during night flight operations aboard the amphibious assault ship USS *Bonhomme Richard* in the Philippine Sea in February 2017. (US Navy)

A VMA-223 'Bulldogs' AV-8B in the foreground flies in formation with one of the squadron's long-nose AV-8B Plus aircraft, both of which are carrying Litening targeting pods. (USMC)

A VMA-231 AV-8B Plus in high-vis markings, and with bomb mission symbols from Operation *Inherent Resolve* in the Middle East painted below the cockpit, at Marine Corps Air Station Cherry Point, North Carolina, in May 2017. (USMC)

An AV-8B Plus Harrier II pilot assigned to VMA 214 'Black Sheep' carrying practice air-to-air missiles on the outer wing pylons and a Litening targeting pod on the centreline pylon. (USMC)

Above: A USMC student replacement pilot with Marine Assault Training Squadron (VMAT) 203 conducts a vertical landing with an immaculate two-seat TAV8-B Harrier Aircraft during Operation *Angry Birds* over Marine Corps Air Station Beaufort, South Carolina, in 2014. (USMC)

Below: A Lockheed Martin F-35B Lightning II Joint Strike Fighter assigned to VMA-121 'Green Knights' flies next to a VMA-211 'Wake Island Avengers' AV-8B Plus Harrier II during fixed-wing aerial refuelling training over eastern California. (USMC)

CHAPTER 8

Last Landings

As Operation *Herrick* came to an end, the Harrier continued to be involved in evolving technologies and technical upgrades. In December 2008 the UK defence and security company Qinetiq successfully completed trials of its Harrier T.4 XW175 Vectored-thrust Aircraft Advanced Control (VAAC) aircraft onboard HMS *Illustrious,* having completed a total of thirty-nine sorties to demonstrate the company's new Bedford Array visual landing aid system. The trials were conducted as part of a contract with the MoD, designed to improve the stability of the F-35B Lightning II short take-off and vertical landing (STOVL) Joint Strike Fighter (JSF) aircraft that will replace the UK Harrier fleet in rolling landings.

Compared to a standard vertical landing, JSF recovery requirements to ships with a 60-knot airspeed approach and landing method, referred to as Ship Rolling Vertical Landing (SRVL), extends engine life by reducing propulsion system stress and allowing heavier payloads to be brought back by the aircraft.

SRVL involves a STOVL aircraft executing a rolling landing onto the carrier flight deck, using airspeed to provide wing-borne lift to complement engine thrust. The aircraft uses its own brakes to stop; therefore, no arrestor gear is deployed. The Bedford Array visual landing aid system improves SRVL by collecting data from external passive references and combining it with information in the pilot's Helmet Mounted Display, allowing the pilot to make more accurate decisions on approach to the deck.

However, pilot acceptability remained unresolved up to the early part of the Joint Strike Fighter programme until the US Naval Air Systems Command (NAVAIR) contribution to the programme through the JSF Program Office (JPO), and through a joint targeted programme in support of the Lockheed Martin F-35B.

Even before the decision was taken to end all UK Harrier operations, Qinetiq's two-seat Harrier T.4 XW175, Vectored-thrust Aircraft Advanced Control (VAAC), was conducting trials to improve the stability of the Harrier's replacement, the F-35B Lightning II aircraft in rolling landings. (Qinetiq)

A No. 1(F) Squadron Harrier GR.7, part of Joint Force Harrier, landing on light aircraft carrier HMS *Illustrious* prior to joining Operation *Orion* in 2008 in the Indian Ocean region. (Crown Copyright)

A Harrier GR.7A in the foreground and a Harrier GR.9 of No. 1(F) Squadron conduct a fly-past of HMS *Illustrious* during Exercise *Joint Warrior* in 2008. (Crown Copyright)

No. IV(AC) Squadron Harrier GR.7s, with ZD470 specially marked, on the deck of HMS *Illustrious* during the build-up to Excercise *Saif Sareea* off the Oman coast in September 2001. (Crown Copyright)

A pair of No. 3 Squadron Harrier GR.7s based at RAF Laarbruch, Germany: new-build ZG861 is in the foreground, with an RAF VC.10 K.3 behind, over the Andes en route to FIDAE'94 in Chile. (David Oliver archives)

A No. 20 (R) Squadron Harrier GR.9, ZD327, originally a GR.5, in the later grey colour scheme, firing a salvo of CRV-7 rockets at a live-firing range. (BAE Systems)

A formation of No. 1(F) Squadron Harrier GR.7. ZD465 is in the foreground while No. 20 (R) Squadron GR.7 ZD375 is flanking an early production 1 Typhoon FGR.4 in 2006. (Geoffrey Lee)

An excellent plan view of No. 800/801 NAS Harrier GR.7 ZD406, showing the big wing, under-wing pylons and refueling probe. (BAE Systems)

The end of JFH's *Herrick* commitment coincided with the last phase of the GR.9 upgrade programme, which included revised software to allow weapons training missions to be flown without the need to carry a captive training round, since the aircraft's own software was now able to emulate the weapon system and enabled full control over the Thales Digital Joint Reconnaissance Pod (DJRP). Other upgrades included the Harrier Advanced Mission Planning Aid (HAMPA) and the integration of Saturn secure communications. The final phase of the programme was to provide network-enabled capability through Link 16, and Variable Message Format (VMF) data link with the integration of the Tactical Information Exchange Capability (TIEC) to enable Harrier GR.9 pilots to join the digital battlefield. Design authority clearance for these upgrades was planned for mid-2011, with delivery of an operational capability by the end of 2012.

2010 was set to be a busy year for post-Afghanistan JHC, with No. IV(AC) Harriers taking part in Exercise *Red Flag* in Nevada and six No. 1(F) Squadron aircraft embarking on the UK's Fleet flagship, HMS *Ark Royal*, for the first time in a considerable period and participating in Exercise *Auriga*, a two month-long carrier deployment in waters off the eastern seaboard of the United States and Canada. However, it was also the beginning of the end for Joint Force Harrier.

Only six weeks after returning from the United States, No. IV (AC) Squadron was disbanded on 31 March, although the historic number plate was passed on to the Harrier Operational Training Unit (OTU), No. 20 (R) Squadron at RAF Wittering, which became No. IV(R) Squadron. In September, No. 800 NAS headed for Cyprus to take part in the four-week bi-annual Exercise *Harding Flame* to gain day and night CAS training with Army unit and Joint Tactical Air Controllers (JTAC), who played such a vital part in Harrier operations in Afghanistan.

As the exercise came to an end, the long-awaited outcome of the UK's new Coalition government's Strategic Defence and Security Review (SDSR) was about to be revealed in October 2010.

Many defence pundits had predicted that if the two new Queen Elizabeth-class aircraft carriers were cancelled, as would be the STOVL version of the F-35 Lightning II, and JFH's day would be numbered. If the carriers and the F-35s were not cancelled, JFH would continue to maintain the UK's carrier strike capability for at least another decade. In the event, both JHF and the carrier HMS *Ark Royal* were to be sacrificed.

At 11.55 hours on 19 November, off the coast of Newcastle, a Joint Force Harrier GR.9 landed on the flight deck of HMS *Ark Royal* for the last time. As announced in the UK SDSR, Joint Force Harrier's fleet of aircraft was to be retired on 14 December 2010 and HMS *Ark Royal* decommissioned in April 2011.

The Harrier's last sixteen-ship fly-past from RAF Cottesmore took place on 15 December, but sadly few people on the ground witnessed this historic flight due to the overcast weather. As a postscript, only five days after HMS *Ark Royal* was decommissioned on 12 March 2011, the UK launched Operation *Ellamy* as part of an international coalition to enforce a Libyan no-fly zone in accordance with a United Nations Security Council Resolution.

The first of
forty-three
production
British Aerospace
Harrier GR.Mk.5
aircraft, ZD318
was assembled
at Dunsfold in
1986 and issued
to the Defence
Evaluation and
Research Agency
(DERA) at
Boscombe Down.
(BAE Systems)

The second
Harrier GR.5,
ZD319 was also
assigned to
DERA. It is seen
here wearing
high-visibility
trials markings
and carrying an
experimental
man-carrying
EXINT
pod. (David
Oliver archive)

Harrier GR.9
ZD320, a
converted GR5
aircraft, replaced
the earlier DERA
trials aircraft
at Boscombe
Down in 2007.
(BAE Systems)

A No. 233 Operational Conversion Unit (OCU) Harrier GR.5, ZD327 is seen in its early green camouflage scheme, based at RAF Wittering. (David Oliver)

Green camouflaged Harrier GR.5 ZD343 is seen conducting trials carrying five 1,000 lb GP bombs on the outer and mid-pylons and the centerline pylon, and Sidewinder AAMs on the inner pylons. (BAE Systems)

Harrier GR.5 ZD407 of No. 1 (Fighter) Squadron (which converted to the type in 1989) is seen flying over the Lincolnshire countryside close to its base at RAF Wittering. (BAE Systems)

Above: Two Harrier GR.7s belonging to No. IV (AC) Squadron are fitted with two 25 mm Aden cannons that were discarded on aircraft deployed to Operation *Herrick*. (David Oliver archive)

Below: No. IV (AC) Squadron Harrier GR.9 ZD330, an upgraded GR.5, is seen armed with Raytheon AGM-65 Maverick air-to-ground tactical missiles (AGM) designed for Close Air Support, and two Aden cannon. (Geoffrey Lee)

A pair of new-build Harrier
GR.7s of No. 1(F) Squadron,
ZG859 and ZG480 in the
foreground, over the North Sea
en route to their base at RAF
Cottesmore in March 2008.
(Philip Stevens)

An RAF Harrier GR.7 of
No. 20(R) Squadron armed
with twin 25 mm Aden cannon
and based at RAF Wittering is
pictured flying above the clouds.
(Crown Copyright)

On board HMS *Ark Royal*,
Harrier GR.7 ZD330 from the
Naval Strike Wing (NSW)
is raised on a hangar lift in
preparation for taking part in
Operation *Joint Warrior* in 2010.
(Crown Copyright)

Left: Two-seat Harrier T.10 ZH663 of No. 20(R) Squadron, based at RAF Wittering, armed with CVR-7 rocket pods in a vertical climb. (Crown Copyright)

Below: No. 1(F) Squadron's T.10 dual-control advanced trainer for pilots proceeding to the full operational Harrier was fully combat capable and could be used in front-line service. (David Oliver archives)

On a dull day off the coast of Newcastle on 19 November 2010, the first of four Joint Force Harrier GR.9As, ZG477, wearing No. 1(F) Squadron Anniversary fin marking, lands on the flight deck of HMS *Ark Royal* for the last time. (David Oliver)

The third aircraft to land on HMS *Ark Royal* on 19 November 2010 was No. 800/801 NAS Harrier GR.9A ZG506, which led the last Harrier fly-past at RAF Cottesmore on 14 December 2010. It is finished in a Harrier GR.1-style camouflage. (David Oliver)

The message in the cockpit of No. 800/801 NAS Harrier GR.9A ZG506, which was piloted by Lt Chris 'Casper' Roy on 19 November 2010, when it landed on HMS *Ark Royal* for the last time. (David Oliver)

The last aircraft to land on HMS *Ark Royal* on 19 November was No. 800 NAS Harrier GR.9 ZD351, originally an early production GR.5. (David Oliver)

Climbing out of No. 800 NAS Harrier GR.9A ZG506 for the last time on 19 November 2010 was Lt Chris 'Casper' Roy, who, in 2014, became an exchange pilot with the US Marine Corps, flying the F-35B Lightning II. (David Oliver)

The last four Harrier GR.9s to be parked on the flight deck of HMS *Ark Royal* in November 2010, with ZD351 wearing a special No. 800 NAS marking on the tail. (David Oliver)

The last Harrier GR.9 to launch from HMS *Ark Royal* on 24 November was ZG506, flown by Lt-Com. James 'Blackers' Blackmore, who, in 2016, became the Royal Navy Fixed Wing Commanding Officer at RNAS Culdrose. (Crown Copyright)

The Joint Force Harrier's last sixteen-ship formation took place over an overcast East Anglia on 14 December 2010, led by JFH Commander Group Captain Gary Waterfall in the camouflaged GR.9A ZG506. (Crown Copyright)

On 19 March 2011, RAF Tornado GR.4s flew from RAF Marham on a bombing mission to Libya to begin a long NATO-led campaign against Colonel Gaddafi's armed forces. It was the sort of operation that UK Joint Force Harrier had been designed for. To add insult to injury, on 31 May 2011 the United States Marine Corps (USMC) announced that it had returned a squadron of AV-8B Harrier II combat aircraft to Kandahar Airfield in Helmand Province to assume full responsibility for providing support for Afghan and ISAF operations throughout southern Afghanistan, exactly two years after the UK Joint Force Harrier was withdrawn from the theatre.

In November 2011, the UK MoD announced that it had agreed the sale of the final seventy-two extant single-seat and two-seat Harrier airframes and associated parts – to be used as a major source of spares for the US Marine Corps fleet of AV-8B aircraft – in a deal that was reported to have been worth around $180 million (£116 million). The aircraft had been kept in storage at RAF Cottesmore, where they had been maintained in an airworthy condition in readiness for sale.

However, they were transported to the 309th Aerospace Maintenance and Regeneration Group (AMARG) at David-Monthan AFB, Arizona, during 2012, where most of the airframes remain to this day, stripped of engines, avionics and mechanical components with no indication of their long-term future. Rotting in an Arizona desert is a sad end for such an iconic British aircraft.

RAF Cottesmore-based No. 800 NAS Harrier GR.9 ZD470 high over RAF Akrotiri in Cyprus in September 2010 during Exercise *Harding Flame*, shortly before the iconic aircraft was decommissioned. (Crown Copyright)

No. 1(F) Squadron two-seat Harrier T.10 ZH665, the last of thirteen built at the BAe Warton factory, flies alongside a IV(AC) Squadron Harrier GR.7, based at RAF Cottesmore. (Philip Stevens)

This immaculate No. 1(F) Squadron Harrier GR.9, ZG508 was withdrawn from use at RAF Cottesmore on 15 December 2010 and delivered to the 309th Aerospace Maintenance and Regeneration Group (AMARG) at David-Monthan AFB, Arizona, in April 2012. (David Oliver)

CHAPTER 9

Overseas Operators

Due to the embargo from the West and ideological solidarity with the Soviet Union, throughout the 1950s the People's Republic of China (PRC) had carried out most of its foreign trade and the supply of military hardware with the Communist bloc. Following the Sino-Soviet split in 1960 as a result of political differences, trade with Eastern Europe declined and China began to look to the West for its imports.

British industry, led by the aviation sector, had attempted to secure business exporting to China, and in 1964 a deal had been struck to allow for the sale of six Vickers Viscount airliners to China for civilian usage, followed by a contract to supply thirty-six DH Trident jet airliners. This marked the formation of a relationship between China and the British aviation industry, notably with Hawker Siddeley and Rolls-Royce, which was to become mutually beneficial to both countries during the PRC's 'opening-up' period in the 1970s.

The Chinese first enquired about the acquisition of the Harrier during the handover of the first Trident aircraft in 1972, expressing interest in the purchase of as many as 200. But discussions between British and Chinese officials stalled, and by the end of the Heath government in 1974, no firm offers had been made to buy the aircraft.

The political turmoil in China that followed the death of Mao Zedong in October 1976 placed the Harrier discussions on hold, as diplomatic relations between the PRC and UK cooled. However, during a visit by a UK business delegation in November 1977, Chinese Vice Premier Wang Chen announced to the delegates that China, 'Intends to acquire the Harrier.'

This declaration of interest was followed by a visit to the UK by Chinese Minister of Foreign Trade Li Chiang later that month, with the main intention of securing the export of military equipment. By November 1978, Chinese interest was made explicit by Vice Premier Wang Chen on a visit to the UK. After receiving a demonstration of Harrier's capabilities, Wang submitted a technical document outlining precisely the Chinese requirements for the Harrier and announced that it was now time for specific proposals.

The indecisiveness of the British government throughout 1978 essentially meant that the Harrier sale to China would not take place. It appeared that domestic considerations for the British government were subordinate to the wishes of the United States during this period.

It was not until 1996 that a Harrier was delivered to the People's Republic of China, when the late Mark Hanna arranged an exchange with the Beijing Air and Space University Museum, where Harrier GR.3 XZ965 in No. IV (AC) Squadron colours is on display.

In fact, the only export contract for British Harriers came in 1977, when the Indian government approved plans to acquire the Sea Harrier FRS.1 for the Indian Navy. Prior to this, there had been reported rumours of a potential Indian purchase of the Soviet V/STOL-capable Yak-36. The Hawker Sea Hawk was phased out from the Indian Navy service in 1978 in preparation for the purchase of Sea Harriers. In November 1979, India placed its first order for six Sea Harrier FRS.51 fighters (to replace its Hawker Sea Hawk) and four T.60 two-seat trainers, the first of which arrived at Dabolim Airport in December 1983 and were inducted into service the same year. Ten more Sea Harriers were purchased in November 1985 and eventually a total of thirty Sea Harriers were procured: twenty-five FRS.51s for operational use and the remainder being two-seat trainer aircraft. Until the 1990s, significant portions of pilot training was carried out in Britain due to limited aircraft availability.

Above: The first of
the initial batch
of twenty-three
Hawker Sea
Harrier FRS.Mk.51s
for the Indian
Navy, G-9-478 is
wearing the 'White
Tigers' insignia on
the tail, seen in
the hover at the
1982 Farnborough
Air Show.
(BAE Systems)

Left: The Indian
Sea Harrier FRS.51,
G-9-487, used for
weapons carriage
trials in the UK,
carrying drop
tanks and anti-ship
missiles in 1982.
(BAE Systems)

The introduction of the Sea Harrier allowed for the Indian Navy's aircraft carrier, INS *Vikrant*, the former HMS *Hercules*, to be extensively modernised between 1987 and 1989 and the Sea Harriers operated from both INS *Vikrant* and again from the former Falklands veteran HMS *Hermes*, which had been sold on to India and renamed INS *Viraat*. As well as the British anti-ship Sea Eagle missile, the Sea Harrier FRS.51s were armed with the French Matra Magic missile for air-to-air combat, 68 mm rockets, runway-denial bombs, cluster bombs and the podded 30 mm Aden cannons.

In 2003 the Indian Navy took delivery of two former RAF Harrier T.4 trainers, which were upgraded to T.60 standard.

In 2006, the Indian Navy expressed interest in acquiring up to eight of the Royal Navy's recently retired Sea Harrier FA.2s in order to maintain its operational Sea Harrier fleet. Neither the Sea Harrier FA2's Blue Vixen radar, the RWR or the AMRAAM capability would be included as certain US software would have had to be uninstalled prior to shipment. However, by October 2006 the deal was cancelled and the Indian Navy embarked on an upgrade programme of fifteen Sea Harriers in collaboration with Israel by installing the Elta EL/M-2032 radar and the Rafael Derby medium-range air-to-air BVR missile. By 2009, accidents had reduced the Sea Harrier fleet from the original thirty to twelve, and the Indian Navy was planning to introduce larger aircraft carriers that could operate Russian MiG-29K carrier-borne fighter aircraft.

The Sea Harriers operated from INS *Viraat* for the last time on 6 March 2016 and on 11 May a ceremony was held at INS, at Dabolim in Goa, to commemorate the phasing out of Sea Harriers from INAS 300 'White Tigers'. Sea Harriers and MiG-29Ks performed an air display at the ceremony, marking the final flight of the Sea Harriers in the Indian Navy.

The first export order for Harriers came from Spain, when nine McDonnell Douglas-built AV-8S Matador Is and two two-seat TAV-8As entered service with No. 8 *Escuadrilla* of the Spanish Naval Air Arm based at Rota in 1976, designated VA-1 and VAE-1 respectively. The AV-8S Matador I was capable of operating from the Spanish Navy's aircraft carrier *Dédalo*, which was the former Second World War-era light aircraft carrier USS *Cabot*.

Spain, already using the AV-8S Matador I, also became the first international operator of the AV-8B Harrier II by signing an order for twelve aircraft in March 1983. Designated VA-2 Matador II by the Spanish Navy, this variant is known as EAV-8B by McDonnell Douglas. Pilot conversion took place in the United States. On 6 October 1987, the first three Matador IIs were delivered to Naval Station Rota in Spain and deliveries were completed by 1988, three of which were subsequently written off.

Two Indian Navy Sea Harrier FRS.51s, IN608 and IN606, of INAS 300 'White Tigers' operating from the carrier INS *Viraat* formate with the US Navy F/A-18F over the Sea of Japan in 2007. (US Navy)

Ground crew servicing an INAS Sea Harrier FRS.51 aircraft on the carrier INS *Viraat*, the former Falklands veteran HMS *Hermes*, while taking part in the multilateral Exercise *Malabar* 2007 in the Pacific. (US Navy)

INAS 800 'White Tigers' Sea Harrier FRS.51 IN614, which was delivered in July 1990, being positioned on the flight deck of the carrier INS *Viraat*. (Simon Watson)

Sea Harrier FRS.51 IN607 – seen here in its faded original colour scheme at its home base INS Hansa at Dabolim in Goa – was one of the original batch delivered to the INAS 800 in 1984. (Simon Watson)

INAS 800 'White Tigers' Sea Harrier FRS.51 IN603 – seen here in a weathered grey overall grey colour scheme taking off from INS Hansa – was the third to be delivered in December 1983. (Simon Watson)

The two-seat Harrier T.60 IN651 was the first of four trainers to be delivered to the Sea Harrier Operational Flying Training (SHOFTU), formed as part of INAS 300 in April 1990. (Simon Watson)

Harrier T.60 IN656, a former RAF T.4 modified with FRS.51 avionics, was assigned to INAS 552, which replaced SHOFTU in 2005, for ab-initio training on the Sea Harrier. (Simon Watson)

Above: Built by Hawker Siddeley and assembled by McDonnell Douglas, eleven Harrier Mk.54/ AV-8Ss were delivered to the Spanish Navy as VA-1 Matadors. (Francois Prins archive)

Below: A Spanish Navy AV-8S Matador in flight over the Spanish aircraft carrier *Dedalo* (the former USS *Cabot*) in 1988. (US Navy)

Above: A Spanish Navy AV-8S Matador armed with twin 25 mm cannons and 2-inch rocket pods parked on the flight line at Naval Station Rota in 1977. (US Navy)

Right: A Spanish Navy AV-8S Matador I flying with the aircraft that would replace it, one of twelve McDonnell Douglas EAV-8B Matador IIs delivered in 1988. (Geoffrey Lee)

BAe test pilots cleared the Spanish Navy's new aircraft carrier *Príncipe de Asturias* (which, unlike the *Dédalo*, had a 12 degree ski-jump ramp) for Harrier II operations in July 1989. It was originally planned that the first unit to operate the aircraft would be the No. 8 *Escuadrilla* but this unit was disbanded on 24 October 1986, following the sales of its AV-8S Matadors to Thailand. Instead, No. 9 *Escuadrilla* was formed on 29 September 1987 to become part of the Alpha Carrier Air Group to operate the EAV-8B.

In March 1993, under the September 1990 Tripartite MoU between the United States, Italy and Spain, eight EAV-8B Plus Matadors were ordered, along with a twin-seat TAV-8B. Deliveries of the Plus-standard aircraft started in 1996, and in May 2000 Boeing and the NAVAIR finalised a contract to remanufacture Spanish EAV-8Bs to bring them up to Plus standard. Boeing said the deal required it to remanufacture two EAV-8Bs, with an option for another seven aircraft; other sources say the total was eleven aircraft. The remanufacture allowed the aircraft to carry four AIM-120 AMRAAMs, enhanced the pilot's situational awareness through the installation of new radar and avionics, and provided a new engine. Eventually five aircraft were modified, the last having been delivered on 5 December 2003.

Spanish EAV-8Bs joined Operation *Deny Flight*, enforcing the UN's no-fly zone over Bosnia and Herzegovina, although Spain did not send its aircraft carrier to participate in the Iraq War in 2003.

In 1993 the Spain ordered eight radar-equipped EAV-8B Harrier II Plus aircraft to be operated by No. *9ª Escuadrilla* on the light aircraft carrier *Príncipe de Asturias*. (McDonnell Douglas)

Spanish Navy EAV-8B Plus were deployed with the NATO forces in Operation *Deny Flight* over Bosnia and Herzegovina in 1993 and numerous NATO maritime exercises. (US Navy)

In 2003, five of the original batch of Harrier IIs had been upgraded to EAV-8B Plus standard, which included a new fuselage manufactured by Boeing, an upgraded Rolls-Royce Pegasus 408 engine, and AN/APG-65 radar. After another was written off, the four legacy EAV-8Bs were again modernised in 2012 by EADS CASA, now Airbus Defence and Space, under a Spanish Navy Upgrade (SNUG) programme with a more powerful Rolls-Royce 408A Pegasus engine and improved avionics comprising a new computer display, the capability to carry the Litening Pod, night vision cockpit, an improved RWR system and Hi/Lo Gain NWS. The Angle Rate Bombing System (ARBS) was retained but it lacked that EAV-8B Plus's APG-65 pulse Doppler multi-mode radar in the extended nose.

The Spanish government announced in May 2014 that it had decided to extend the aircraft's service life to beyond 2025, due to a lack of funds for a replacement aircraft. Following the decommissioning of the *Príncipe de Asturias* in February 2013, the sole naval platform from which Spanish Harrier IIs can operate is the *Juan Carlos* amphibious assault ship.

In 1997, Thailand acquired seven AV-8S and two tandem-seat TAV-8S Matadors from the Spanish Navy. The aircraft were obtained as part of a Thai Navy order for an 11,500t Spanish-built light aircraft carrier, HTMS *Chakri Naruebet*. The aircraft carrier was designed to operate an air group of Matadors and helicopters, and was fitted with a ski-jump. However, by 1999 only one Matador was operational, and the entire fleet was withdrawn from service in 2006.

Above: In 1992 the Spanish Navy sold seven of its AV-8S Matador Is to the Royal Thai Navy to be operated from its light aircraft carrier HTMS *Chakri Naruebet*. (Francois Prins archive)

Right: A single AV-8S Harrier is seen on the flight deck of the Royal Thai Navy's Spanish-built carrier HTMS *Chakri Naruebet* in the South China Sea in 2001. (US Navy)

Following a demonstration of the Hawker Siddeley Harrier on the Italian Navy helicopter carrier *Andrea Doria* in the late 1960s, the country began investigating the possibility of acquiring the aircraft. Early efforts were hindered by a 1937 Italian law that prohibited the navy from operating fixed-wing aircraft because they were the domain of the air force. In early 1989, the law was changed to allow the navy to operate any fixed-wing aircraft. However, following a lengthy evaluation of the Sea Harrier F/A.2 and AV-8B Harrier II, an order was placed for two TAV-8Bs in May 1989, followed by a contract for sixteen AV-8B Harrier IIs. The two-seaters, the first to be delivered, arrived at Grottaglie in August 1991. They were used for proving flights with the Italian Navy's helicopter carriers and on the light aircraft carrier *Giuseppe Garibaldi*. After delivery of the TAV-8Bs and the first three AV-8Bs, all subsequent Italian Navy Harrier IIs were locally assembled by Alenia Aeronautica from kits delivered from the United States.

In early 1994, the initial batch of US-built aircraft arrived at MCAS Cherry Point for pilot conversion training. The first Italian-assembled Harrier was rolled out the following year and in mid-January 1995 the *Giuseppe Garibaldi* set off from Taranto to Somalian waters with three AV-8Bs on board as part of Operation *United Shield* to maintain stability following the withdrawal of UN forces.

In 1999, they were used for the first time in combat missions when they were again deployed aboard *Giuseppe Garibaldi*, which was participating in Operation *Allied Force* in Kosovo. Italian pilots conducted more than sixty sorties alongside other NATO aircraft, attacking the Yugoslav Army and paramilitary forces and bombing the country's infrastructure with conventional and Laser-Guided Bombs (LGB).

In 2000, the Italian Navy was looking to acquire a further seven remanufactured aircraft to equip *Giuseppe Garibaldi* and a new carrier, *Cavour*. Existing aircraft, meanwhile, were updated to allow them to carry AIM-120 AMRAAMs and JDAM guided bombs. From November 2001 to March 2002, eight AV-8Bs were embarked aboard *Giuseppe Garibaldi* and were deployed to the Indian Ocean in support of Operation *Enduring Freedom*. The aircraft operated throughout January and February 2002, during which 131 missions were logged for a total of 647 flight hours.

In 2011, Italian Harriers operated from carrier during Operation *Unified Protector* as part of the military intervention in Libya. In total, the eight Italian Navy AV-8Bs flying from *Giuseppe Garibaldi* dropped 160 LGBs during 1,221 operational flight hours.

Italian Navy AV-8Bs are due to be replaced by F-35B Lightning IIs, which will form the air wing of carrier *Cavour* in 2020. The first of fifteen STOVL-versions of the Lightning II was rolled out at the Italian government's FACO at Cameri Air Base on 5 May 2017, which was also the first F-35B to be assembled outside the United States.

Four USMC AV-8B Harrier IIs on the flight deck during initial trials of the type on the aircraft carrier *Guiseppe Garibaldi* before the Italian Navy's aircraft were delivered in 1994. (Italian Navy)

Above: Fourteen AV-8B Harrier II Plus aircraft are operated by the Italian Navy's *Gruppo Aerei Imbarcati* 'The Wolves'. (Francois Prins archive)

Below: An Italian Navy AV-8B Harrier II Plus recovers to the carrier *Guiseppe Garibaldi,* carrying the AIM-120 Advanced Medium-Range Air-to-Air Missiles (AMRAAM). (Francois Prins archive)

Above: The flight deck crew secures an Italian Navy AV-8B Harrier II Plus with 'The Wolves' head symbol below the cockpit on the *Guiseppe Garibaldi* in the Mediterranean Sea in 2015. (US Navy)

Below: A flight deck crew member signals to the pilot of an Italian TAV-8B Harrier II aircraft aboard the *Guiseppe Garibaldi* as the aircraft carrier takes part in Exercise *Dragon Hammer* '92. (US Navy)